Epsom Coaches

A driving force since 1920

Roy and Andrew Richmond

ACKNOWLEDGEMENTS

*Our very grateful thanks go to the following people who have provided
assistance with the production of the book.*

Gordon Allis
David Brooks
Maurice Doggett
Andrew Dunsmore/Picture Partnership
Geoff Heels
Motoring Heritage Centre, Alexandria, Scotland
Peter Lemon
John Simons
Steve Stevens-Stratten
Volvo Bus Limited

*And to the many members of staff, customers and suppliers who have
contributed to our success and long standing since 1920*

First published: 2002
ISBN: 1 900515 65 2
Published by: DTS Publishing PO Box 105, Croydon CR9 2TL
         in conjunction with H. R. Richmond Limited, Epsom, Surrey KT19 9AF
© H. R. Richmond Limited
Printed by: Unwin Brothers, The Gresham Press, Old Woking, Surrey GU22 9LH
British Library Cataloguing in Publication Data. A catalogue record for this book is available from the
British Library.

Epsom Coaches
A driving force since 1920

CONTENTS

No. of Certificate.

239398

REGISTRATION OF BUSINESS NAMES ACT, 1916.

CERTIFICATE OF REGISTRATION.

I 𝔥𝔢𝔯𝔢𝔟𝔶 𝔠𝔢𝔯𝔱𝔦𝔣𝔶 that a Statement

of particulars furnished by

Herbert Roderick Richmond

in the business name

"Richmond & Reeves"

of :- 38a, High Street, Epsom,

pursuant to Sections 3 and 4 of the above-mentioned Act

was registered on the 11th day of January 1927

Dated this 14th day of January 192 7.

Registrar of Business Names.

Section 6 of the Act enacts that, if a change occurs in *any* of the particulars registered, such change must be notified to the Registrar on the prescribed form within 14 days of its occurrence. The Board of Trade may, on application, allow an extension of the period within which such notification must be made.

Section 13 enacts that, if a firm or individual registered under the Act ceases to carry on business, the partners of the firm, or the individual (or if he is dead his personal representative) must give notice thereof to the Registrar on the prescribed form, within three months after the business has ceased.

Section 11 enacts that Certificates issued under the Act must be kept exhibited in a conspicuous position at the principal place of business.

Forms of notification of change or cessation may be obtained from the

REGISTRAR OF BUSINESS NAMES, SOMERSET HOUSE, STRAND, LONDON, W.C.2.

Although the business commenced in 1920, this certificate formally registering the name is the earliest official record so far traced

INTRODUCTION

We thought it would be of interest, especially to local people, to provide an account of the development of Epsom Coaches throughout the years. The Company, which recently celebrated its eightieth birthday, grew from the pioneering spirit of Herbert Richmond and his business partner Jim Reeves, running charabancs and horseboxes from their High Street garage.

Our book has taken several years to write, and covers the development of the business up to the present time, as well as a section describing some of the unusual characters, and strange incidents that have occurred over the years. For the transport enthusiast we have also included a listing of all the buses and coaches owned by the Company since 1920.

Regrettably, there are very few family-run businesses remaining in Epsom, although companies such as Bowdens still have a strong presence. The butcher, baker, grocer and other tradesmen who have all served us well in the past have been unable to survive in today's competitive world.

Throughout its life, the business has been under threat, yet it has managed to survive the Second World War, nationalisation, fuel rationing, and the constant pressure from competition. The Company's longevity comes from a range of factors, including the good staff relationships that have been constant throughout its life, the foresight to see changes in the market, and the ability to meet those changing needs.

During its life, the Company has operated horse transport, retail travel agencies, local bus services, a tobacconist shop, as well as its core business of operating coaches. In the pages that follow, we will be explaining the reasons for each change in direction, and outline the Company's present position.

Roy and Andrew Richmond

Herbert Roderick Richmond

Chapter 1
THE FORMATIVE YEARS

Herbert Roderick Richmond, better known as Roddy, was born on 31st August 1891, and was the youngest son of Frederick and Clara Richmond. Frederick Richmond was a farmer in the village of Reepham in Norfolk. Roddy's brother was a qualified doctor, and his sister was an accomplished pianist who had regular engagements throughout Austria and Germany.

Roddy went to Chapmans Academy, a boarding school in Norwich, where he went through the indignity of being a "fag", attending to the needs of a house prefect. On market days, his father would go to Norwich to buy and sell sheep, and this gave them an opportunity to meet up occasionally during term time. His father was used to dealing in cash for these transactions, a habit that Roddy and to some extent, Roy followed in later years. The practice ceased when Roy took his trousers for dry cleaning one day without checking his pockets!

During the school holidays Roddy used to repair the farm machinery out in the fields. He always carried a gun to keep down the rabbit population, an activity he kept up until the outbreak of the Second World War. With his interest in mechanics, it was decided that Roddy, aged 15, should take up a five-year apprenticeship with Argyll Motors Limited, a car manufacturer based in Alexandria, Scotland. He took up lodgings with a Miss Primrose and her brother, who were regular worshippers at Sunday Chapel, and he soon became accustomed to the Scottish way of life.

Argyll Motors was established in 1899, originally manufacturing components for the bicycle industry. They produced their first light car in 1899 at a price of 155 guineas, and went on to produce reliable cars that were exported throughout the world. The company competed in almost every Reliability Trial going. Amongst the trials, W G Scott, driving alternately with his colleague, L C Hornsted, drove a car round Brooklands for fourteen hours without problems, averaging 72.59 miles per hour and completing the run at 8 o'clock in the evening, with only two punctures. The new 15/30 Argyll broke world records and its achievements were reported nationally.

The year before Roddy joined the company, Argyll Motors started the construction of an ambitious new factory aimed at producing 3,000 cars per annum, the largest in Europe. The new factory, opened by Lord Montague of Beaulieu, cost £250,000 to build and was lavishly constructed with hand carved stonework on the façade, and gold leaf to the dome encasing the top. The high cost of the building and the downturn in sales would eventually place the company in liquidation. The façade is still to be seen today, fronting the Lomond Factory Outlet and Motoring Heritage Centre in Alexandria.

It is worth noting that at the time Roddy was an apprentice with Argylls, there were two other apprentice mechanics working together, namely John Logie Baird and Oliver Hutchinson. The two had become great friends, both joining the Army in the 1914-18 War. They met again later and worked on what was then the dream of television. Each played their part, Baird being the brains and Hutchinson the energy. The first demonstration of television in 1926 showed Hutchinson's face.

Roddy Richmond's apprenticeship with Argyll Motors started in 1906, and involved a year in the tool room, a year in the assembling department, a year in the car repair department, one and half years in the finishing and testing department, and 6 months in the Edinburgh Repair Depot. He stayed with Argylls and in January 1914 became Foreman of their Repair Works in Albion Street, Leeds, leaving there in September 1914 when Argylls went into liquidation.

During his time with Argyll Motors, Roddy Richmond's work included road testing the cars, and instructing their use to customers. His customers included Sir Harry Lauder, the popular singer and entertainer who was noted for the songs *Roamin' in the Gloamin'* and *Keep Right on to the End of the Road*. On one occasion in 1911, Roddy delivered a Fire Engine to London at an average speed of 30 miles per hour. He was very disappointed when Argylls had to abandon development of their steam driven car, as he was convinced that it had a future.

After a short spell of duty as a Sergeant with the Royal Engineers, stationed at the Curragh (Ireland), Roddy was drafted to Ruston and Hornsby in January 1916, working on aircraft production as a fitter. During his time with the Company he was

THE ARGYLL CAR
IS SO SIMPLE.
I'M SURE IF YOU GO WRONG
FATHER WILL NEVER KNOW
I'VE HAD IT-AND BESIDES
HE'S SO PLEASED WITH IT,
HE COULDN'T BE CROSS
WITH ANY BODY
JUST NOW

HAVE A TRIAL RUN

We will fix a date with pleasure. The driver will stop and start on the steepest hill. Some firms will not allow this test.

ARGYLLS, LONDON, Ltd. (Telephone 2641 Gerrard),
17, NEWMAN STREET, OXFORD STREET, W.

A.B.C. CODE (FIFTH EDITION)

REPAIR WORKS
AND GARAGE,
BUTTS COURT,
ALBION ST.

ARGYLLS,
LIMITED.

TELEGRAPHIC ADDRESS,
ARGYLLS, LEEDS.

J.S. MATTHEW,
MANAGING DIRECTOR.

SHOWROOMS,
86 ALBION STREET,

LEEDS.

TO WHOM IT MAY CONCERN

30th September 1914.

We have pleasure in stating that Herbert R. Richmond has been in the employ of this Company as Foreman of our Repair Works, from the 15th January 1914 to the 30th September 1914. Mr. Richmond is an Expert Mechanic, and we have always found him to be a steady, reliable, and industrious man. He is accustomed to handling men, and to anyone requiring a good all round Foreman, we can thoroughly recommend him as a suitable man with considerable experience.

ARGYLLS LIMITED

GEN. MANAGER

transferred to the Inspection Department as a viewer, and was given complete charge of the department in April 1917, leaving there in July 1919. He then joined The Air Navigation and Engineering Company at Addlestone, Surrey as Chief of their Inspection Department.

On 10th February 1919, Roddy Richmond married Bessie Harriet Reeves at Poplar in London. On 1st April 1920, he went to work at Sopwith Aviation Company Limited in Kingston, and on 4th August that year, the couple had their first child, John Roderick Richmond, better known as Jack. With aircraft production suffering a downturn after the First World War, on 10th September 1920, workers at Sopwith Aviation received the following notice:

Bessie Harriet Richmond in the uniform of a State Registered Nurse

We much regret we find it impossible to reopen the works as the difficulties by restricted credit prevent the Company from finding sufficient working capital to carry on the business and it will therefore be wound up.

G H Mitchell – Works Manager

Following the loss of his job at Sopwith Aviation, Roddy made the decision to go into partnership with his brother in law, Jim Reeves, forming the business of Richmond and Reeves. They needed a considerable amount of courage to start up in the transport business as they risked losing their savings in the process.

The business started operating from Wernham's Yard to the rear of Boots the Chemist in Epsom High Street, now the location for the Lifestyle Centre. The premises had a very narrow frontage with access to a larger plot of land to the rear. The entrance was obstructed by protruding chimneystacks, which reduced the approach to the yard. The accessibility was also made worse as the High Street was narrower in those days, and adjacent shopkeepers had to raise their shop blinds to allow vehicles into the yard.

The entrance extended to about 65 feet deep, with Parr's newsagency and Tutte's confectionery shops on either side. Wernham's blacksmith shop was situated behind Tuttes, and there was a ladies hairdressing saloon behind Parrs. Beyond that a brick building large enough to garage and maintain two vehicles, and a drawing board type of desk with space for a diary and telephone. Further down the yard there were sheds occupied by Boots the Chemists, and a Dutch barn type of building with corrugated asbestos sheets, backing on to the railway embankment. The horseboxes, charabancs and coaches were parked in the barn. Even in those days a town centre address was comparatively expensive.

In the beginning, Roddy would commute from Kingston by motorbike, but he soon moved into an upstairs flat in East Street to be nearer the business. The flat, incidentally, was owned by Miss Ede, sister of Chuter Ede, who later became Home Secretary in the Attlee Government.

Entrance to the High Street garage - notice board on the left shows the name Richmond & Reeves

One of their first vehicles was an ex-army Lancia charabanc that cost £200 to buy from the War Department sales at Slough, and they spent a further £300 in parts to restore it. The charabanc bodywork cost £386 bringing the total cost of the vehicle to £886. In 1921, the partners bought a further Lancia chassis with a Warwick charabanc body, at a cost of £366. According to the Company accounts, the fleet grew steadily, with the addition of two Thornycrofts in 1922; a further Lancia and Thornycroft were added in 1925. The partners were also believed to

PB 8058 – one of the early Lancia charabancs

Beano during the 1920's

have operated A.E.C., Reo, Straker Squire and Crossley vehicles during the 1920's.

The telephone number in those days was Epsom 555, which was subsequently changed to 5252, 25252, 725252, and has now been replaced by 731700. In the early days, the Epsom telephone exchange was still manual, and it was commonplace to have wrong numbers and long delays waiting for the operator to answer. The office system also had a handset and a switchboard that enabled calls to be transferred between the garage and Mr Richmond's house, just over a mile away. A hand-cranked generator on the switchboard at the garage would produce enough current to ring the bell at the house, and thereby transfer the call. Although Epsom had been the first exchange to be updated in the 1920's, it was one of the last to go automatic in 1960.

Between 1920 and 1930 passengers travelled by charabanc. The layout of charabancs was similar to that of a toast rack, with rows of wooden bench seats, and a door for each row. Charabancs were normally converted from ex-army lorries used during the First World War. Although passengers were not that comfortable, they were at least covered by a canvas roof when it rained. The driver, on the other hand, would have an open windscreen and be entirely exposed to the elements. Roddy Richmond used charabancs solely as passenger vehicles, although some operators used them as a lorry during the week, and converted them into a charabanc at the weekend. Mr Richmond operated both horseboxes and charabancs, so the drivers were expected to drive either type of vehicle.

Charabancs were mainly used to convey racegoers to meetings. They would

Straker Squire charabanc in Epsom High Street

Bill Tinker standing by his Model T Ford charabanc in 1921

travel to Sandown, Kempton Park, Hurst Park, Lingfield, Brighton and Ascot. Epsom Brotherhood and Epsom Town Football Club would also hire charabancs for their away matches. There were quite a large number of servicemen convalescing in St Ebbas and Horton Hospitals, and the charabancs would be used to take them to various functions such as garden parties and London theatres.

During the 1920's, the Company carried out one of their first extended tours,

This picnic is typical of the parties arranged by Kate Foale, whose father, Mr Chambers owned the knitting wool and toy shop opposite the garage

Lancia PB 8058 now with modifications (see page 11), including electric lighting

which lasted three days. They were hired to pick up a party from Clapham Common and take them to the Catherine Wheel in Henley. The following day they drove around the Buckinghamshire countryside visiting Marlow, and on the final day they returned to Clapham. The charabanc driver, Bill Tinker, was extremely pleased to receive a ten-shilling tip, which was very good when you consider he earned 25 shillings a week.

Charabancs would not normally go out after dark, as the lighting was very poor. The headlights were especially dim when the engine was idling, becoming brighter when the engine revs increased. This was due to the fact that the vehicles didn't have batteries, and the power for the lights came directly from a commutator driven by the engine. The side and rear lights were lit by oil, and would frequently go out. The engines had to be cranked by hand.

Lighting was so poor that on one occasion a charabanc ran off the road whilst carrying a wedding party to Newmarket. The party, including the bridegroom, had to help pull the vehicle back on to the road in almost complete darkness.

On one occasion Bessie Richmond was travelling on a charabanc with her mother-in-law as it struggled to climb Reigate Hill. During the ascent her mother-in-law noticed the red-hot silencer through a gap in the floorboards, and said in a loud voice "Bessie, we are on fire". In an attempt to keep the matter quiet Bessie responded, "Keep your voice down, nothing to worry about".

Whilst awaiting the completion of one of his charabancs, Mr Richmond learned that the coachbuilder's business was about to go into liquidation. A Mr Bundy from Reigate called at Mr Richmond's house to tell him that if he didn't collect

An AEC charabanc – possibly B-type lorry chassis – was purchased in 1924 for the grand sum of £215

the vehicle that evening, the liquidators would impound it.

The first excursions during the period 1920-1930 were unhampered by licensing, and Mr Richmond made up parties of friends, or by chalking up the details on a blackboard outside the High Street garage. These outings were comparatively expensive at one pound for a day return to Brighton, or from half a crown to three shillings and six pence to a local race meeting. The higher fares reflected the cost of longer journeys where poor road surfaces and hills such as Bury, Duncton and Reigate increased the risk of breakdowns.

Another charabanc of Richmond & Reeves – also believed to be an AEC B-type – seen on a seaside outing

Chapter 2

THE PRE-WAR YEARS

Harriet gave birth to their second child, Roydon Bircham Richmond, on Wednesday, June 1st 1925 (Derby Day) in a private Nursing Home in College Road, Epsom. Roydon was the name of a hamlet in Norfolk, where Roddy had lived, and Bircham was the maiden name of his grandmother Clara. Roddy, not to be outdone by the birth of his son, brought a new charabanc along to the nursing home, so that Bessie could admire it, babe in arms, from the upstairs window!

Jack Richmond, meanwhile, started his education at Miss Gray's Lecture Hall School in Station Road (now Upper High Street), which is the present site of the Odeon cinema. He then attended Epsom County School for Boys, which is now Glyn Grammar. He was a popular boy who sang in the choir, and was a member of the Scout Group attached to St Martins Church, Epsom. Despite his good intentions, his parents later discovered that he had been playing truant from both of these activities.

The Heads of Epsom County School for Boys and Rosebery County School for Girls had a strict policy of their pupils not fraternising in public when in school uniform, so Jack would catch up with his friends when he could, and the three cinemas were favourite meeting places.

Whilst living in Miles Road, the family had been used to travelled by motorbike, with Bessie in the sidecar and Jack on her lap. In 1928 they moved to a house in Copse Edge Avenue, which they named Booton after Roddy's childhood home in Norfolk, Booton Hall. They also purchased their first car, an Austin Chummy, the

Reo saloon coach outside garage to the rear of Epsom High Street
the small boy in the picture is Roy Richmond

Adult Education Institute, formerly Epsom County School for Boys

first in a line of new cars, many of which were of American origin - Buick, Essex, Hudson and Packard, all weather saloon cars with right hand drive. The family would take an annual holiday to Scotland and keep in touch with the business by collecting mail at pre-arranged Post Offices on route (Poste Restant).

In 1930, Roy's education started at the Lecture Hall School. At the age of ten, he passed the entrance examination and joined his brother at Epsom County School for Boys in Church Street, now an Adult Education Centre. The School was divided into two buildings, the present Adult Education Institute and a converted store to the rear of Absalom & Garland, the local ironmongers. Roy recalls that on occasions the Headmaster would send a pupil to Nuthalls, the general stores across the road, to buy a cane for him to administer "six of the best".

During school holidays, Roy would go down to the garage in the High Street and he recalls playing against the railway embankment at the back of the Boots Car Park. The embankment had been created to enable Epsom railway station to be connected, via the East Street bridge, to the Victoria and London Bridge line in 1924. There was also another station and goods yard in Upper High Street.

During the prolonged General Strike of 1926, Roddy drove a charabanc to London every day for six months. It was in the same year that Roddy's partner Jim Reeves died; the Company continued as Richmond & Reeves until H R Richmond Limited was formed in 1933. The Company traded as Epsom Coaches throughout.

Mr Richmond bought his first saloon coach in 1929, an Albion with a 32-seat body manufactured by London Lorries (acquired by Duples in 1932) on an Albion chassis, registration number UU5955. Another Albion, a Gilford and five shorter Bedford chassis, accommodating 20 to 26 passengers were also built over the following years at Hendon. The fleet consisted of six coaches and six horseboxes until the outbreak of War.

In 1930, Roddy Richmond claimed the licence to operate Express Services. The licence required the Company to operate the services irrespective of the number of passengers booked. They ran during the summer period only, daily to Brighton and Worthing, and twice weekly to Southsea and Bognor. There were also a few other services to race meetings beyond the Metropolitan Police District,

Epsom High Street during widening

to Windsor and Lingfield. Even after the grant of these licences, annual return forms had to be submitted in order to establish that there was still a need for the services, with a profitable return to the operator. In the 1930's a day trip to Brighton cost 4 shillings and sixpence (22½p). Although it was on their doorstep, the Company was denied the right to operate the local service from the Station to the Epsom Racecourse on race days.

In 1934, following the decision to widen Epsom High Street, Mr Richmond was forced into finding alternative premises as he only held a short-term lease. He moved to Trower's granary opposite Mount Hill in South Street, and sub-let part of the granary yard to Alf and Ralph Scragg, who were corn merchants supplying fodder to most

EPSOM COACHES - DAILY SERVICE

TO SEPTEMBER 30th.

	MONDAY TO FRIDAY			SATURDAYS AND SUNDAYS		
	Single	Day Return	Period Return	Single	Day Return	Period Rct.
BRIGHTON -	4/6	5/-	8/-	5/-	6/-	9/-
WORTHING -	5/6	6/-	9/-	6/6	7/-	10/-
				Single	Day Return	Period Ret.
BOGNOR (Tuesdays & Fridays) -				—	7/-	10/-
SOUTHSEA (Wednesdays & Fridays)				6/-	7/-	10/-

ALDERSHOT TATTOO	ASCOT RACES
4/6 each day	Tuesday and Friday 5/6
Except Saturdays 5/-	Wednesday and Thursday 7/-

On Period Bookings Date of Return must be specified when Booking. Children in arms under three years carried Free
Children under 14, Two-Thirds Full Fare. Full Seat allowed.

RICHMOND & REEVES, HEAD OFFICE, High St., EPSOM

Proprietor : H. R. RICHMOND.   Telephone : EPSOM 555.

Advertisement circa 1930

Epsom Coaches' South Street Garage – near the site of Epsom Playhouse

of the racing establishments in the district. In his youth, Roy recalls helping Alf thresh the oats.

Uden & Company completed the conversion of the existing granary buildings. On part of the wide frontage, two lock-up shops were built, one was let out to a boot and shoe repairer, and the other became a coach hire and ticket office, as well as selling cigarettes and tobacco. The decision to sell cigarettes from the office made it even harder for Roddy to break his habit of smoking 60 a day. He had taken up his mother's habit, except that she smoked Woodbines, and lived to the grand age of 93! In those days a packet of 20 Players cigarettes cost just under a shilling (5p).

It is also worth commenting on the passing trade of tramps, who Roddy referred to as roadside inspectors. On occasions, they would buy a packet of snuff or twist on their way to the Dorking Road Workhouse, and ask him to look after their savings until the next morning. The reason for this was that if they were found to have more than a shilling on them, their money would be confiscated. In fact, it was known that some tramps would hide their money in Rosebery Park overnight, and collect it the following morning. There may still be some hidden treasures there!

Although maintenance was carried out in rather austere conditions on the ground floor, Mr Richmond commissioned Uden & Company to build a proper workshop and stores in the roof of the original outer granary, accessible by way of a spiral staircase.

A pulley could hoist heavy machinery, parts and tyres through a space covered by removable floorboards when not in use. The workshop was quite spacious with a four metre long bench and room to store spare parts, reconditioned engines and a lathe.

There was always a lack of space for parking vehicles, so a barn in Heathcote Road was rented from Canon Chrystall for thirteen guineas a quarter to accommodate three 32-seater coaches from about 1933 to 1939, and again from 1948 to 1953, when they were given notice to make way for the building of the Catholic Church Hall, which has since moved to Mount Hill. Pre-war, one of the coaches was parked in a barn at the bottom of Tot Hill in Headley, and another two coaches were parked at the rear of Dorking High Street.

When Jack left school, his parents felt he should have achieved better results and they sent him to a College in Chancery Lane, but he didn't take kindly to his academic life. He worked for Clerical Medical Insurance in High Holborn for a while before becoming Assistant Registrar for Births, Deaths and Marriages at Ashley House in Epsom. During his two years in the post he also helped his father out each morning before going to work, by driving school children from Langley Vale to Lintons Lane School in a 7-seat Vauxhall car. He soon discovered to his cost, there was a 30 mph speed limit in Ashley Road!

In those days, when Mr Richmond required a large number of coaches he would hire in from other operators such as Graves of Redhill, and Adnams of Merton both of whom had fleets of 30 coaches or more. There were also other smaller

Epsom Laundry outing in Waterloo Road, Epsom, during the 1930s

operators, such as Kahn of Leatherhead, and Egelton of Merton, who both had similar size fleets to Richmonds. There was a good relationship between the companies and they would all help each other, when needed.

Larger outings required as many as eight coaches, and these were typically hired by the Conservative, Liberal or Comrades Club, or one of the local churches to take their Sunday School children on their annual outing. Roy recalls going on an outing from Upper High Street (Station Road as it was then known), and seeing a line of coaches stretching from the junction of the High Street in readiness to take them on their day out. In those days, the side windows could be wound down and the party would give a loud cheer as they went through the villages, and locals responded with a wave.

On occasions Roddy would have to drive one of the horseboxes to a race meeting and sometimes during his youth, Roy would accompany him. After setting down the horses, they would make their way into the nearest town, as they had little interest in racing.

In 1937 Jack Richmond volunteered to become a Territorial in the Royal Engineers at Stonecot Hill, along with a number of his friends. He attended some weekday evenings, weekends, and a summer camp.

Jack Richmond
Territorial in the Royal Engineers

Roy Richmond, meanwhile, was attending Epsom County School for Boys, which was transferred to Ewell in 1938. A year later, war was declared and underground air-raid shelters were built in the school grounds, where pupils spent a good part of their school life. Roy left school immediately after his sixteenth birthday as there seemed little point in going up to the sixth form to re-sit his School Certificate.

Prior to the introduction of saloon coaches, vehicles were very basic and drivers could spend a great deal of their time at a destination preparing the vehicle for its return journey. Solid tyres were replaced by tubed tyres, which were unreliable. They not only punctured because of the poor road surfaces, but also due to the poor quality of the tubes and valves. The driver would be responsible for

22

PK 7883, an Albion PM28 with 29-seat Duple coachwork incorporating roof luggage storage

repairing any punctures and it was usual to carry two spare wheels. By 1930 saloon coaches were taking the place of the charabanc.

Coaches were not very powerful in those days, and could only just make it to the top of Bury Hill, on the Littlehampton road, provided they had a clear run. The passengers were more enclosed than they had been in the charabancs, and were given travel rugs to keep themselves warm during the winter months, as there was no heating.

Before luggage lockers were built into the rear of the coach, the driver placed the baggage, or crates of liquid refreshment, depending on the type of group, on the roof. There was a set of retractable steps at the rear corner of the coach for the driver to climb. If the group were not providing their own refreshments, it was customary to stop at public houses. Roy has seen as many as 30 coaches parked on the forecourt of the Black Swan at Pease Pottage, taking a break on their way to Brighton. If the passengers wanted to make their own arrangements or have just a comfort stop, the driver would choose somewhere suitable where there were trees and undergrowth. The ladies would go to one side of the road, and the men to the other.

During the winter months the vehicle radiators had to be drained every night, as there was no anti-freeze. In the morning, the drivers would have to refill the radiator with hot water, which helped thin the engine oil, and ease starting. The driver would have to use the starting handle and crank the engine by hand.

In a half-cab coach, the driver was isolated from his passengers and the only means of communication was via the sliding window behind him. They retained

some of the characteristics of the charabanc by having a sliding roof section that allowed passengers the opportunity of being exposed to the elements. Although the driver kept warm from the heat of the engine during winter, his cab could become unbearably hot in the summer. To enter the cab, the

PK 7883 again - from the front

driver would use the stirrup step provided, or step onto the top of the front offside tyre. Driving mirrors were very small, and when reversing, the driver had to open his cab door and look back over his shoulder. One driver fell out whilst reversing at Cheddar Caves, luckily another driver saw his predicament, and managed to jump into the cab and apply the handbrake!

Racegoers, referred to as punters by the drivers, travelled on the excursions as often as six days a week. Their bookings were accepted by telephone, sometimes using a nom de plume, which Roy recognised when passengers boarded the coach in the South Street garage, or at the Foresters Hall in Waterloo Road. There was always a cross section of punters, including two retired matrons, bookmakers with blackboards to write their odds on, and tipsters who managed to extract their fare from the unsuspecting public at the racecourse, earning enough to pay the driver on the return journey. It must be remembered that there were no betting shops or television in those days.

The regulations applying to coach hire meant that customers were not allowed to publicly advertise the trip if they collected individual fares, although societies were allowed to promote trips through club newsletters. Coach hire has become far less regulated, and the type of clientele has changed. Today's business is much more likely to come from a tour operator, business, club or organisation, than an individual. Weddings have carried on much the same throughout the years.

Jack Richmond was at the Territorial Summer Camp in 1939 when war broke out, and he went straight into service, civilian life had come to an abrupt end.

Chapter 3
THE WAR YEARS

By the outbreak of the Second World War the business consisted of six horseboxes and six coaches, however, the Army commandeered all but one coach. A sergeant came to the South Street garage with the appropriate requisition order to take the vehicles. Roddy, accompanied by Roy, drove one of the vehicles to the Barracks in Church Street, Kensington.

Following the loss of most of his business, Roddy drove the remaining 32-seat Albion throughout the war years. He would convey schoolchildren between Kingswood and Tadworth, as well as Langley Vale and Epsom; take workmen to bombsites; transport wounded soldiers to and from Horton Hospital; and later on, German Prisoners of War to work. After the evacuation from Dunkirk, Roy recalls watching convoys of wounded soldiers being taken by coach from Epsom Downs Station to Horton Hospital. The coach windows were removed for safety purposes.

At the age of 19, Jack Richmond was stationed with the Royal Engineers at various farms near East Grinstead in Sussex. They were responsible for maintaining mobile searchlight and generator units, used to target enemy aircraft.

Roy, now aged sixteen, went for an interview at the Westminster Bank in Epsom. He started work in the Epsom Branch, and the experience taught him a great deal, especially as many of the male staff had been called up for war service, and that meant taking on jobs that would not normally have been open to him.

Roy was often sent out on relief to other branches, sometimes at a minutes notice, including Tadworth, Worcester Park, Ashtead, Cheam and Teddington. In Tadworth sub branch, there was little to do, so Roy spent much of his time studying for his bank exams. The sub manager was a pretty relaxed kind of chap and, on one occasion when the bank inspectors made a surprise visit, he was barely visible through the clouds of pipe smoke.

Roy Richmond

Security was not such a problem in those days, and Roy recalls taking a Gladstone bag, filled with cash, up to the Tadworth branch on the 406 bus in time to open at 10 o'clock. Unlike today, cash was handled in a very open way, copper and silver would be exchanged locally with other banks, and this involved pulling a trolley along the pavement with the bags stacked one on top of another. During wartime, £5 notes and higher denominations were withdrawn from circulation as they were considered a possible means for black market operations; the policy also discouraged the printing of counterfeit notes by the enemy.

On Quarter Days, Roy would have to work to ten or eleven at night and on the 31st December until midnight, despite having to open as usual the next day. The manager used to live over the premises in Epsom, and one of the juniors would have to sleep there for security purposes when he went on holiday. Roy recalls staying one night over the Christmas period.

Mechanisation in banks was limited to little more than an adding machine. The manager and chief clerk, along with their staff, were required to check the 2000 customers' current account balances, recorded in the ledgers. All vouchers for the day's transactions had to be dispatched by post that evening, come what may. Most cheques were cleared at Stoke-on-Trent, and the banks own credits and debits were dispatched to Chard, Somerset. Cheques drawn on local banks were cleared locally each day at the close of business by an exchange taking place at a bank in rotation, Barclays, Lloyds, Midland, National Provincial or Westminster.

The Westminster Bank was by far the busiest bank in Epsom, and in the early 1940's held accounts for the Town Hall, the Post Office, and all five local mental hospitals. Ledgers were hand written and had to be taken downstairs at night to the strong room, either by placing them on the trolley and using the manually operated lift, or carrying two or three ledgers at a time, down the stairs. The ledgers were very heavy and the lift worked by winding a 30 inch diameter wheel to convey the trolley to and from the strong room below. These tasks fell to the junior who had to do it for a year, before relinquishing the task to the next junior. Statements were hand written, although pass books were still in use for a few privileged customers.

Apart from his banking duties, Roy was on a rota to do a night's fire watching in a segment of the town from the Bank to the Post Office. He was detailed to be with two ladies who kept the china shop two doors away, and they would sit in deck chairs amongst all the china waiting for an air raid. When the air raid warning sounded, Roy was on his feet in no time at all and outside the shop. If a bomb had dropped, he thought there was a better chance of survival outside, rather than inside amongst the china.

After Dunkirk, there was a clamour to join The Local Defence Volunteers, nicknamed "The Broomstick Army" due to their lack of real weapons. It later became known as the Home Guard, when Lee Enfield rifles replaced the

Jack Richmond.
Pictured at home in Copse Edge Avenue

broomsticks. The television comedy Dad's Army is based on the Home Guard, and Roy felt there was a great deal of truth in the episodes written by Perry and Croft. Roy likened himself to character Private Frank Pike whom Captain Mainwaring had to suffer, however Roy's mother didn't come chasing after him with his scarf!

On Sundays, the Home Guard would fix bayonets and jab at a palliasse hanging from the ceiling, or walk across the open playing fields of Epsom College, exposing themselves to the imaginary enemy. There might have been a purpose in learning how to use a rifle in the College indoor range, and spending nights out at Home Farm on the borders of Headley, or Epsom Racecourse, but on reflection, Roy wonders really how effective they would have been in action.

After two years of comparative inactivity in the Army, Jack Richmond volunteered for the RAF, and became a trainee pilot. He learnt to fly a Miles Magister trainer, with the help of the Thames Valley as a navigational aid! Very soon after completing the course he was on his way by a "Queen" liner across the Atlantic to the Southern States of America where he learnt to fly heavy bombers from various American airfields, before returning home. He took over a Wellington bomber as Sergeant Pilot and was stationed at Benson-on-Thames, and in Lincolnshire, preparing for the nightly raids over Germany. Tragically, Jack was killed during a mission on 2nd May 1943, when his aircraft exploded, taking all lives on board. Roy recalls answering the doorbell and receiving the telegram with the devastating news.

Jack had been engaged to marry Leonora, who he had been attracted to during the morning breaks at school. In the Depot Road school, Jack would glance up at Leonora on a balcony above The Quadrant shops, reminiscent of the story of Romeo and Juliet.

Jack's funeral took place at St. Martins Church, Epsom and he is buried in the War Graves Commission Section of the Ashley Road Cemetery. His name appears on the Rolls of Honour at Glyn Grammar School, and H M Registrar General.

After three years in the bank, Roy became enlisted in the Army in the spring of 1944, having passed Part 1 of the Institute of Bankers examinations, which served

Roy Richmond (fourth from left in the back row) at Catterick.

him well in the years ahead. He joined the Suffolk Regiment at Bury St. Edmunds and carried out his Primary training there, still dressed in his Home Guard uniform for the first six weeks, because they couldn't find a uniform that fitted. During his time in the bank, his weekly pay had risen from one pound ten shillings to two pounds five shillings, however, in the Army, he earned three shillings a day with board and lodging included.

Throughout his Army life, due to his height, Roy had the doubtful privilege of marker when drill or parades were taking place. This made him more conspicuous, especially when sloping and presenting arms with rifles. Like everyone else, he soon learnt to get out of bed immediately at six o'clock reveille; otherwise the Corporal would soon tip them out, complete with palliasse, onto the floor.

Most of their training took place on Bury St Edmunds Golf Course where they crawled around on their stomachs and learnt how to become infantrymen. At the end of the six weeks he signed up for his preferred Corps or Regiment, and was fortunately accepted for the Royal Corps of Signals.

Roy joined his Corps at Catterick Camp and for the next six months learnt how to operate Morse Code, field telephones, teleprinters and signal procedure. Rosters included one night a week on duty at the Guard Room, two hours on and four hours off, during which time it was impossible to sleep. Another weekly duty was spent "spud bashing" which occurred more often if their bed inspection was below standard. Church Parades took place every Sunday morning. An exercise on the Yorkshire Moors gave him a taste of things to come with his next posting. He passed the appropriate Army trade of Operator Keyboard and Line.

Having completed his training at Catterick, Roy went on embarkation leave, which coincided with Christmas, and returned to St Anne's on Sea, where he spent a month on the famous Golf Course and endured a toughening up process with night operations. He remembers forty men huddled round two Tangye stoves trying to keep warm in their damp clothes, whilst billeted in a long Nissen hut. Once a week they went to Blackpool and had a fish and chip supper, or tripe and onions for those used to such delicacies. There were also swimming lessons at Lytham Baths, which was part of the preparation for Draft ROZHH. He was quite sure they were bound for an Arctic climate.

One Sunday morning, the Corps went by train from Lytham to Preston and then to Greenock. They boarded the *ss Highland Brigade*, an all purpose freight and troop carrier that had originally been used for the Argentine meat trade. The Wireless Officer, John Beckwith, recognised Roy when boarding the ship, and made himself known before setting sail that evening - he lived in the same road as Roy, Copse Edge Avenue, Epsom.

There were 120 soldiers on board the *ss Highland Brigade*, and they were responsible for looking after 1,400 German "U" boat prisoners of war. They sailed down to Holy Loch and had to wait six days for a convoy. Setting sail, they met up with nine destroyers and another merchant ship, although they didn't know their destination. Messages were passed from ship to ship by Aldis Lamp, during periods when there weren't any Germans on deck. The prisoners were allowed 10 minutes on deck a day under the Geneva Convention rules.

The soldiers on board thought they were passing Northern Ireland, and that their destination was Canada, so it came as a surprise to arrive in Gibraltar. During the voyage, Roy developed a raging toothache and a non-commissioned officer in the Royal Army Medical Corps volunteered to make the extraction. He sat him down in a wicker chair, gave him the necessary injection, and to his great relief extracted the right tooth. To this day he is not sure whether he was a qualified dentist.

The *ss Highland Brigade* continued along the North African coast, eventually arriving in Port Said, by the Customs House where they disembarked. They were given the job of taking the prisoners to a Compound in the Western Desert. Roy recalls the Germans

Roy Richmond in Maadi

29

Roy Richmond hitchhiking to Ismailia

singing their national anthem, and "We March against England".

Having discharged the prisoners, they took a train to Cairo stopping at Zag a Zig, Quassassin and Tel el Kebir, each station having a plaque noting General Gordon's battles. They arrived in Cairo on King Farouk's birthday which was the first occasion that the blackout had been lifted, and everyone was in party mood. Roy recalls being driven down Kasr el Nil with horns blowing, and a general razzmatazz. It was not easy to negotiate the streets of Cairo, and King Farouk was usually driven through the town at speed, as he was not very popular and could have been assassinated. As history unfolded, he was deposed.

Roy's next stop was Maadi, where he was stationed for the next two years. Maadi was a dormitory and transmitter site for GHQ Middle East. Eight of them shared a tent which had been excavated to a depth of about four feet and the whitewashed walls were built from River Nile mud, about six inches thick. There was a gap between the walls and the canvas roof, which provided an occasional breeze, even if it was warm air from a "kamseen" wind. The desert had extreme temperatures from the cool nights to the hot days. Each man was issued with nine blankets and they used their greatcoats for extra warmth in the winter.

In the three years Roy spent in Egypt, it only rained once, however, it made up for lost time. Being situated on the edge of an old wadi (river), the rain soon flooded the Camp and most of their personal belongings and equipment were lost. The storm was so severe that it washed away the sand beneath the railway and left some of the sleepers suspended 25 feet in the air. The railway had been built as a Base Camp for the Kiwis in the Western Desert Campaign.

Roy's life was centred around the Signal Office of GHQ Cairo at Grey Pillars in the Garden Suburb and being a trained keyboard and line operator, his first spell was shift work in the teleprinter room with communications to the whole of the Middle East from Tripoli and Benghazi to the west, Khartoum in the south, and Jerusalem, Basra and Tehran to the north and east. When climatic conditions, or sabotage, prevented the use of teleprinters, messages were ciphered and sent by wireless.

The war had not finished in the Far East and the Atom Bomb was yet to come. For many of those soldiers who had been in Egypt four years or more, time had come for them to be sent home, but Roy remained in Cairo, despite concerns that he might be posted to Burma.

VE Day on May 8th went by with little to celebrate until VJ Day in the August. The General Election made little difference to their way of life, and being a young enlisted soldier, Group 60 meant there would be a delay of two years before they were able to return home for good. Roy was fortunate enough to go on leave to the UK, by means of Medloc, a route that took him across France from Toulon to Calais.

During his three years in the Middle East life wasn't too unpleasant, but he never really got used to the flies, the heat and the various smells, especially the stench of the sewers when they were opened up at night.

In Cairo, there were two good canteens, "A Hole in the Wall" and "Music for All" where soldiers could have a bath in luxury, or they could visit the air-conditioned Metro cinema. They would also go to Cairo Cathedral; a modern building that was well attended by local residents and army personnel.

Roy made two journeys into Cairo each day, either going via the banks of the Nile and within sight of the Pyramids, or occasionally through the Dead City, which became part of Cairo in more recent times, and there were people actually living within the tombs. Part of his duties in Camp and in the Signal Office required the employment of local labour, which was paid at the rate of 10 Piastres a day, the equivalent of ten new pence. It was no wonder that buckshish (backhanders) were part of the Arab way of life! Roy learnt Arabic colloquially, at least enough to make himself understood.

Laundry, known locally as "dhobi", was no problem, as they could do their own underclothes, but shirts were more difficult as they needed starching. The village had more than enough "fellahin" (locals) wanting to do it. The main form of payment was cigarettes, which were issued once a week in tins of fifty. The Arabs would set up their own little villages next to the Camp. Once a week, kit inspection would be cancelled to allow for a de-bugging session, which required a liberal application of paraffin to prevent the termites.

Roy Richmond in the uniform of the Royal Corps of Signals

On his return from duty one day, Roy forgot to take in his greatcoat and it was stolen. This was a disciplinary offence and an army form 252 was issued against him. His cap was removed, and he was marched into the Commanding Officer, who knew exactly what had happened, he was fined £1.

About this time, the Sergeant Major discovered Roy had been a bank clerk before joining up, and transferred him to the Company Office for a number of months, to sort out pay. A married man or a soldier supporting his mother, had a substantial sum deducted from his pay, leaving him with the equivalent of eighteen new pence a day. Roy was earning the equivalent 60 pence a day by then, without deductions, and so comparatively well off, and not having to pay Mess fees. The conduct of some Officers and Senior NCO's left a lot to be desired and he preferred to remain a Corporal and refused further promotion.

The Sergeant Major was an ignorant man, very pompous, who told him on occasions to issue a 252, an army charge sheet. On one occasion, Roy corrected a grammatical error with the result that the Sergeant Major short-listed him for a transfer to PAIFORCE (Persia and Iraq Command). He packed his kit bag, and was on his way via Jerusalem, when he was called back by the Commanding Officer to resume normal duties.

The British Army had been in Egypt for over a century and the Egyptians were seeking their own independence. A decision was taken to retire to the Canal Zone, where Roy spent the last six months of his Army life in Fayed, by the side of the Bitter Lakes. He could see ships assembling to form a convoy to pass through the Suez Canal, as it was only wide enough for one-way traffic.

The war had been over nearly two years, and many servicemen were growing restless and near to mutiny. Eventually Group 60 came up and Roy was on his way from Port Said to Liverpool by the *ss Andes*. So Corporal R B Richmond left the Army and was discharged at Aldershot in 1947, returning to civilian life and changing his Army Pay Book containing details of courses, medicals and leave, for the return of his civilian Identity Card.

Chapter 4

THE POST-WAR YEARS

The Second World War effectively brought a halt to the development of coach travel, and the business didn't really recover until the mid 1950's. Despite the war, in 1944 Mr Richmond managed to buy a new 32-seat Bedford Duple Utility bus with wooden bench seats, thus making a fleet strength of two. Even after the war, coach operators were rationed to one or two new vehicles a year, which restricted expansion for some time. The choice of vehicles in the post-war period was limited, and resulted in the Company purchasing a variety of makes with chassis from AEC, Austin, Crossley, Maudslay, and bodywork from Duple, Plaxton and Whitson.

By the end of the war, Roddy Richmond was in poor health and felt that after six years of running the business alone, he wanted to retire, or at least take things easier. His eldest son Jack had died as a bomber pilot in the RAF, and Roy was still serving in Egypt. Nevertheless, Roddy continued to work, and built the coach fleet back up to four vehicles - the Albion that he had driven throughout the war,

OPF 331, an AEC Regal III, by Epsom Grandstand in 1950.
35-seat coachwork was by James Whitson & Co.

a utility wooden-seated bus, and two austere 29 seat coaches. He also purchased six second-hand horseboxes, which needed a lot of attention.

On his return from war service in 1947, Roy decided to help his father run the family business. In the following year, he married Doris Law at Christ Church in Epsom, and they set up home in Ewell. In the coming years they had three children, Christopher, Andrew and Rosemary.

During wartime, and in the years that followed, there was fuel rationing. The Company had no choice as far as fuel suppliers were concerned and they had to use the nearest Pool depot. Although fuel was rationed for private hire work, petrol for advertised services was given a far higher priority and the Company soon re-commenced operating the Brighton and Worthing service daily during the summer months.

When rationing ceased, the Pool depots closed and the major suppliers such as Regent Oil Company, Power Petroleum, Shell, BP and Mobil started offering supply contracts, which offered rebates of approximately one penny per gallon. To induce customers, the oil companies would also give out small free gifts including book matches, which seemed a strange gift considering the product they were selling. Jet Petroleum was a new entrant to the oil business and gained business during a general tanker drivers' strike, by defying the strike call. Their action eventually ended the strike and Epsom Coaches remained loyal to them for some time afterwards.

In those days, business was carried out on a far more personal basis than today. Suppliers' representatives would call on a regular basis regarding the purchase of coaches and horseboxes, petrol and oil, insurance, motor spares and even carbon paper. Suppliers have had to cut back on the personal approach, and most business is now transacted by phone, fax, letter or e-mail.

Drivers' working hours were unrestricted, and they worked long hours, rarely getting days off during the summer season. Nowadays, legislation strictly controls the amount of rest drivers have, and tachographs have been introduced to keep track of this information. Random checks are also carried out by the Department of Transport.

Apart from the long hours, drivers would also have to clean their vehicles inside and out. They needed to be extremely flexible and be prepared to drive either a horsebox or a coach, whereas nowadays they could still be asked to drive a coach, or perhaps cover one of the local bus routes. Drivers' duties were eased in the late 1960's when the Company introduced its first automatic vehicle wash. In the mid 1990's it also introduced the use of cleaning contractors for the interior, which has helped make conditions for Epsom coach drivers probably the best in the industry.

Traditionally, drivers have undertaken other duties during the winter period including essential vehicle and building maintenance work. In the 1960's, drivers such as Ernie Warwick and Ken Lifford, both of whom had a good mechanical knowledge, ably assisted the full-time mechanic, Emil Renggli. Despite the seasonal nature of the business, the Company has never had to resort to laying drivers off during the winter, although some worked on a seasonal basis.

TPE 550 – Bedford SBG with 35-seat Yeates coachwork

One of the longest serving employees, Albert Wall, stayed with the Company from 1922 until his retirement in 1963. When he started, his weekly wage was £3, and the speed limit was only 12 mph. On one occasion he was caught breaking the speed limit by 3 mph, and was fined five shillings. Roy recalls another incident when Albert phoned from Clapham Common to say that his coach had dropped into a hole in the road with 33 passengers aboard. The Council hadn't placed any hurricane lamps around the road works, and there were no streetlights. Luckily nobody was injured and the party managed to get to the theatre by underground before the curtain went up.

The South Street garage had two shops in the front, and at one stage both of them were leased to Jack Garrett, a local shoe repairer. One of the shops was later demolished to make way for a larger entrance, and an additional room was rented next door giving direct access by staircase to the adjoining premises. Following this, another room was also rented to cope with the expansion. The rented offices used another entrance, which was shared by the hairdressers upstairs. Some customers would wander into the coach booking office expecting a 'short back and sides'.

Roddy Richmond built himself an office in the roof of the garage, however, due to the continual running up and down stairs it only survived two or three years. Following this, a ground floor office was constructed using the same framework, and a small flap was inserted into the wall to pass tickets through, or give an invitation to a customer to take a seat in one of the two chairs that filled the small office.

Although active in the business until the late 1950's, Roddy was suffering from the onset of Parkinson's Disease. During his illness, Bessie would encourage him to go to work most days. She would drive him from their home in Copse Edge Avenue to Ashley Road, and he was given a target to walk, in stages, across Rosebery Park to the garage in South Street. She would normally collect him from the garage at midday.

Roddy's love of engineering continued and he spent some of his time constructing a scale model of the 'Royal Scot' locomotive. Unfortunately he didn't manage to complete the project, although it is understood he was able to run the engine using

Roddy's scale model of the 'Royal Scot' locomotive, recently restored by Ron Warren, of Ashtead

*111 CPB – AEC Reliance with 41-seat Yeates 'Europa' coachwork built in 1957.
This vehicle was usually driven by Ken Boxall*

*715 DPD – a Yeates Europa bodied Bedford SB3 leaving Victoria Coach Station
driven by Fred Aston in the late 1950s*

80 JPF – a Bedford SB1 with Burlingham Seagull 41-seat bodywork at the
1959 Brighton Coach Rally driven by Reg Burrows

205 MPG – a Bedford C5Z1 – at the
1960 Brighton Coach Rally driven by Ron Hogsden

TELEPHONE
EPSOM 5252 (3 LINES)

EPSOM COACHES
Inc. LEATHERHEAD COACHES

PROPRIETORS: H. R. RICHMOND LTD
DIRECTORS
H. R. RICHMOND,   B. H. RICHMOND,   R. B. RICHMOND

MOTOR COACH OPERATORS
AND BOOKING AGENTS

37 SOUTH STREET
EPSOM · SURREY

Letterhead used in the late 1950s

compressed air. The model is still in the family's possession, and has recently been lovingly restored by a local model engineer, Ron Warren of Ashtead.

In the mid 1950's, Epsom Coaches acquired the businesses of Bookham Saloon Coaches and E E Law of Leatherhead, which brought the fleet strength up to 20. Bookham Saloon Coaches yard was retained until 1986 when the whole operation was moved to the Epsom garage.

One of Law's drivers, Ken Boxall, transferred to Epsom Coaches and carried out a regular run to Montreux for an existing client. Roddy had been reluctant to take coaches abroad due to the possibility of mechanical failure, but Roy persuaded his father that the opportunities outweighed the risks. Apart from driving, Ken Boxall also undertook most of the coachwork repairs, firstly at the Bookham garage, and subsequently at the Longmead garage.

In the late 1950s, Epsom Coaches operated regular services to Eastbourne, Bexhill and Hastings for 9/6 (nine shillings and sixpence); Brighton for 8/-; Bournemouth for 14/-; Leigh-on-Sea and Southend-on-Sea for 6/9. The Company also offered a wide range of day trips to destinations such as Cheddar Caves which cost 22/6; Salisbury, Winchester and Stonehenge (12/-); and Wye Valley (25/-).

One of Epsom Coaches' regular jobs in the 1950's was to convey the Cambridge Boat Crew from the RAC Club in Epsom to their training sessions on the Thames. This covered a three-week period each year, and culminated in the annual boat race.

Between 1953 and the early 1970's Epsom Coaches employed a skilled Swiss engineer by the name of Emil Renggli. He had previously worked with the Country Area of London Transport, and with Sir Malcolm Campbell on his world speed record holding Bluebird. Emil could make virtually anything, and was the mainstay of the Company's service department throughout the 1950s and 1960s. Being a fellow engineer, Emil got on very well with Roddy Richmond. Emil was extremely

The Cambridge Boat crew warming-up by 590 CPF, a 1957 Bedford 'A4/L7', with Plaxton 29-seat coachwork. The original was signed the crew

touched when Roddy presented him with an airline ticket to visit his ailing mother in Switzerland.

On the driving front, Roy Richmond held a Public Service Licence until 1985. The first time he drove a coach to London was to undertake his Public Service Vehicle Test at 109, Lambeth Road. The test was far less rigorous in those days, and several applicants were dealt with at a time, each one taking their turn at the wheel whilst the others watched on.

It was necessary for Roy to be able to drive a coach, as he was frequently on standby to cover for driver shortages, late running, breakdowns etc. Typically, he would cover a school or works contract starting and finishing with a journey to Wildt's factory in Bookham, the Gala Cosmetics factory in Tolworth, or McMurdos works contract to Beckenham, with a journey to a local school in between. These journeys would often fit around a normal day's work in the office.

Before Roy left the garage each evening, he had to phone the local telephone exchange to refer calls to his home in Ewell. He might still have been called back for an emergency, and he would lay out his clothes before going to bed in case he needed to make a dash back to the office. In later years, when more staff became available, he had the luxury of not having to rush about so much.

The 1960 Tours Programme offered a Special Old Age Pension Week in Margate

for £6 5s 0d inclusive of travel and accommodation. The holiday included a facility ticket, which enabled free use of deck chairs, putting greens and cliff-lift, as well as reduced admission prices to the Winter Gardens, Theatre Royal, Westgate Pavillion, Whist Drives and lower fares on local coach excursions.

In the day tour section for that year, they advertised no-passport day excursions to France by air from Lydd Airport to Le Touquet, priced at 80 shillings. The cross-channel steamer was a cheaper option at 50 shillings; landmarks and points of general interest would be available on the Steamer's notice board!

In 1960, the Company made its first inroads into providing local bus services and applied to operate a service from Tattenham Corner to Epsom Railway Station to compete with London Transport. The service was the idea of Major Gordon Instone, a local resident, who was fed up with the existing service and thought that in conjunction with Epsom Coaches, he could do better. Although the Traffic Commissioner refused the Company's application, the service went ahead in the

Gordon Instone on board

form of a club, paying an annual subscription of a half-crown (12½p), making it possible to collect individual fares. The new service gained a lot of publicity from the media including an article in the Daily Telegraph, and an interview with Major Instone on the BBC's South-Eastern News Service.

The Company acquired Ivy Cottage to the rear of the South Street garage in 1960, and an extension was built to house eight coaches. When the adjoining granary lease expired it enabled the garage to be widened yet again, and the area was used to provide better vehicle maintenance facilities. The fitters now had some warmth in

274 AOU with 41-seat Duple 'Super Vega' coachwork on a Bedford SB8 chassis

the winter, albeit by paraffin blowers, rather than crowding round the Tangye stove in the open yard. At the same time the opportunity was taken to bring the upstairs workshop down to ground level in the new extension. The inner part of the upstairs workshop was also converted to provide the drivers with a rest room, a facility long overdue. Even with the new facility, the staff remained loyal to the Dorking Gate Café opposite.

One night during the 1960's, Roy Richmond received a call from the Police saying that one of his coaches was lying on its side in a hayfield between Headley and Epsom. Roy soon realised the coach should not have been anywhere near Headley. He dressed quickly and drove to the scene to find out what had happened. Just after passing Nower Wood his worst fears were confirmed

H. R. RICHMOND LTD.
37 SOUTH STREET · EPSOM · SURREY
Phone: EPSOM 5252

Tours
1961

Office Hours:
Monday—Saturday: 8 a.m.—5.45 p.m.
Sundays and Bank Holidays: 8.15 a.m.—10.30 a.m.

42

when he saw the blue lights flashing about a hundred yards off the road, and the coach in the field. Apart from the Police car there was a fire engine and an ambulance. Due to a soft landing in the hay, there was surprisingly little damage to the coach and everyone present managed to lift it into an upright position. Fearing the worst, Roy was asked to go to Epsom Hospital to identify the person they had captured in the uncut hay. On entering the ward he was directed to a bed where a man lay fast asleep, obviously recovering from too much alcohol. Fortunately, the culprit was not one of the Epsom drivers, but a drunk who had staggered into the Epsom yard and taken the coach for a joy ride.

Until the tenancy of the granary terminated, there had been deliveries of corn and various other animal foods throughout the day. Even the increased width of the garage meant that only a few vehicles were able to turn round inside. Vehicles that were last in, had to draw up outside the shop, pull across the road and reverse into the garage, which meant stopping the traffic.

A great deal of Roy Richmond's time and effort was spent on acquiring Road Service Licences to extend the Company's range of regular services and tours. Herbert Morrison, Minister of Transport, was the architect of the 1930-1933 Road Traffic Acts, which resulted in putting many small operators out of business, and the creation of large bus groups. The Acts failed in their aim to improve passenger transport and instead, put unnecessary restrictions upon the industry.

From the introduction of the new legislation, all routes and excursions within the Metropolitan Police District required authorisation from the Traffic

384 XPJ – a 1962 AEC Reliance with 51-seat Plaxton 'Panorama Continental' coachwork

43

*532 LOR was a Bedford VAL 14, with 49-seat Harrington 'Legionnaire' cocahwork, bought in 1964.
Driver Stan Robbins*

Commissioners, with the exception of routes covered by the London General Omnibus Company and its successors, the London Passenger Transport Board. The system prevented smaller operators from gaining excursion permits, and Richmonds were only able to operate to three local race meetings – Hurst Park, Kempton Park and Sandown Park.

Richmond's came within the Metropolitan Traffic Area, covering a thirty-mile radius from the centre of London, and controlled by the Commissioner for the area. It was necessary to obtain road service licences for regular services, excursions and tours. Beyond the thirty-mile radius, a Backing Licence was required, to cover the areas South Eastern, Eastern, Western, East Midlands, West Midlands, North Western, Northern, Yorkshire, Scotland and South Wales. The web had tightened considerably and all applications had to be advertised in a publication called "Notices and Proceedings". Following publication, Public Hearings were held allowing objectors to cross-examine the applicants. The scene had been set for monopolies to operate all the major routes from Victoria Coach Station, namely the British Electric Traction Group, and the Thomas Tilling Group of Companies.

The East Kent Road Car Company, Maidstone and District, Southdown Motor Services and British Railways, the successor to the four regional rail companies – Great Western, Southern, London Midland & Scottish and London North Eastern – had the combined might to oppose applications by firms such as Epsom Coaches,

535 LOR, another 1964 Bedford VAL 14 but with 52-seat Harrington 'Legionnaire' body, pictured in Brighton being driven by John May

on the grounds of unfair competition, and that existing services adequately served the public need. If an operator had the courage to file an application to operate at separate fares, it meant briefing a solicitor, and on some occasions Kings Counsel, in order to present the application at a Traffic Court Public Hearing held by the Traffic Commissioner.

The applicant had to present his case at the public hearing, and give good cause, with the support of witnesses and documentary evidence, to show that existing services did not fulfil the public need. Other local operators would also lodge objections, including Surrey Motors of Sutton, Duvals, and Kingston Luxury, companies that had been more fortunate in claiming a foothold when the 1930 Act came into being.

Epsom Coaches picking-up area was confined to Ashtead, Epsom, Ewell and Tadworth and the Company made several applications to increase the number of picking up points. London Passenger Transport Board fiercely opposed the applications, contending that passengers should make their own way to the existing pick-up points using public transport. The objections were not always justified, as customers were not prepared to travel by public transport to join a coach excursion or tour, even in those days.

Roy Richmond would gather up customers, and other contacts to attend the Metropolitan Traffic Commissioner's Public Hearings in London. The supporters would be taken to court, and be cross-examined by Traffic Managers whose sole intention was to discredit them, quite often with remarks or suggestions that they had been paid to come along to the hearing. The hearings were held in Marsham Street and supporters would sometimes have to wait on until 7.00pm for the conclusion, or maybe the case would be adjourned to the next day. Roy remembers a significant breakthrough when Sir Henry Piggott, sitting as the Traffic Commissioner, authorised Epsom Coaches to run to Eastbourne and Hastings, against the might of the monopolies.

Epsom Coaches Road Service Licences expired every three years on the 30th September, and most years they would have to make applications for additions and deletions. The process took nearly three months for the applications to be listed in the Notices and Proceedings gazette, which then allowed objections for a period of 14 days.

These objections were unspecific, quoting, "generally as may be adduced at any Public Hearing held by the Commissioner". This action prevented negotiations prior to the Hearing, and caused further delay until the date of the Hearing was published. Therefore, an application submitted at the end of the summer season could easily take until February for a decision. The consortia of objectors were unwilling to come to an agreement beforehand and it was common practice for one of them to come forward at the eleventh hour and make an approach for a compromise. By that time Roy had briefed Counsel, and incurred a fee.

Another example of restrictive practice was operated by the Isle of Wight operators who banded together and objected successfully in the Traffic Courts to prevent

FAA 554A – Bedford VAM 14 with 42-seat Duple bodywork

mainland operators from bringing their coaches on to the Island. The result was that Epsom Coaches would have to drop off their passengers in Portsmouth, and they would have to join an Island coach to complete their journey.

From 1950 to 1980 as wartime restrictions started to relax, and subject to the limitations of licensing, the choice of destinations grew; however, competition from the family car meant a gradual reduction in the once popular family day out by coach. The result was the Kingston and Sutton operators started to reduce their licensed operations and eventually decided to call it a day. Over a period of time picking-up points in these areas have been included within the one programme for economy of operation.

The scope for offering a wider choice of excursions was limited. The destination quite often had to be disguised by the use of different outward and return routes when advertising separate fares requiring a Road Service Licence. To places such as Tunbridge Wells the title became the Weald of Kent. The overall time was generally restricted to a half-day within a certain radius, to ensure they were not competing with a regular service from Victoria Coach Station.

The Croydon and London based Tour Operators concentrated on tours of five or more days' duration, so Epsom Coaches applied to operate three and then four day tours to Devon & Cornwall, the Lake District, Wales and as far north as Edinburgh. Although successful, a complete breakthrough was not achieved until the late 70's when the objectors realised that de-licensing was about to take place. After fifty years of frustration there were no more hassles, and unnecessary cross-examination in the Traffic Courts. Nowadays, it is unlikely the Monopolies and Mergers Commission would allow these restrictive practices.

Originally, the catchment area for tours was restricted by the licensed picking up points and three booking agents were appointed: Normans Stores in The Street, Ashtead, Williams news

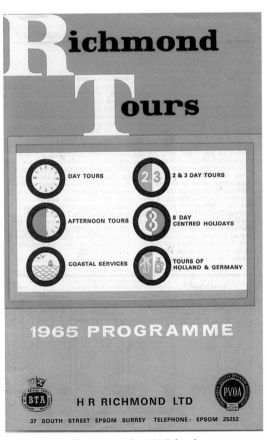

Cover from the 1965 brochure

agency in Ewell High Street, and Chappells in Cross Road, Tadworth. Newsagents generally fulfilled the role of a Booking Agent and they had to be serviced with brochures. There was a regular daily service to Brighton and Worthing from June to September, twice weekly to Bognor and Southsea. These resorts attracted passengers for holidays and the Traffic Commissioner classified these destinations as Express Services allowing single and period return fares as well as for the day. Three of the most popular summer events included the Aldershot Tattoo, Royal Ascot and Goodwood Races. Except for the race meetings throughout the year it was a very intense operation in the summer, with little work in the winter.

The growth of package tours by air meant that tour operators would have to transport their passengers from central London to airports such as Southend, Manston, Luton, Stansted and Gatwick. This required a Road Service Licence, as it was deemed that the road section was part of the inclusive fare. Epsom Coaches applied for a licence to carry passengers to Manston Airport, near Ramsgate. The licence was granted by the Traffic Commissioner, but East Kent Road Car Company were very unhappy and appealed to the Minister of Transport, who overruled their appeal. The Company's determination was costly but rewarding, as it opened the door for other Road Service Licences to Manston. Here again, the East Kent Road Car Company opposed the applications, but at the eleventh hour withdrew, and the licences were issued. Although deregulation took place in 1986, licensing continues under the jurisdiction of the Traffic Commissioner, however, only 42 days notice is required to start or amend a local service.

In 1962, there were 21 coaches in the fleet, ranging in size from 14 to 49 seats. The fleet mileage was 517,000 per annum and the Company had just added two new 36 foot long (11-metre) coaches to the fleet, following the introduction of this new permitted length. The booking office was starting to develop its role as a travel agency and had become agents for Glenton Tours, Le Roy Tours, Friendship Tours, Southdown, Blue Cars, Lyons Tours, Galleon, Scotia and Wallace Arnold as well as selling tickets for its own services. Whilst the Company's day tours were thriving, the coach holiday programme was still in its infancy, and only covered tours to Blackpool Illuminations, and a coach-air excursion to Paris. Tom Pratt managed the booking office between 1953 up to his retirement in 1982. Tom had spent many years in the Fire Service before joining Richmonds and was also well known for his voluntary work for the Sea Cadets unit on Longmead Estate, T S Foxhound.

Coach design was progressing and coaches in the early sixties had an entrance door in front of the axle, instead of behind. With the axle further back, the vehicle's turning circle was reduced, and the passengers could now board within view of the driver, and be seated together.

With the introduction of the roll on, roll off ferries, there was no stopping the flow of vehicles across the Channel, especially with day excursions to Le Touquet. Before the Iron Curtain was lifted, the Company also sent coaches to Poland for the Wimbledon Speedway Supporters Club, and East Germany. The Channel Tunnel is now a popular

NOR 635F – Bedford VAL 70 with Plaxton 'Panorama I' coachwork. Driver is Ken Lifford

alternative means of access to the Continent.

Over the years, some coaches have been produced with three axles in order to cope with additional vehicle weights, but they have never been that popular. The most successful tri-axle vehicle was known as the Bedford VAL, which was 36 feet long (11 metres) and commonly known as a 'six legger'. Epsom Coaches had twelve examples of this model.

One of Epsom Coaches' customers in the 1960's was an excitable Manager of an Italian Tour Operator. One Saturday morning she phoned Roy and said, "I need a coach immediately as my Italian coach is not here, and the group have to start their journey back to Rome today". Roy replied to the effect that the coach driver must be somewhere. "No, he is here, but no coach, it has been stolen". Well, Roy could see there was no alternative but to send a coach to London and start making arrangements to get the party back to Italy. He despatched a driver to London to pick up the party, whilst another was organised to meet up with them half way to Dover, and take them through to Rome. A few days later, it was discovered that the Police had impounded the Italian coach as it had been causing an obstruction. By this time the party had arrived in Italy, and the Epsom driver was on his way back to England. Mrs Venturini was not a happy person!

Apart from leisure travel, very few workers had their own transport, many relying on coaches to take them to work. Most of the large factories would provide daily coach transport for their workers during the 1960's, but during the seventies and eighties most of the factories closed down, or moved out of the area. Epsom Coaches had regular contracts with firms such as Wildts in Great Bookham (four coaches a day), and Gala Cosmetics in Tolworth (three coaches a day). Apart from the area's industrial decline, workers were also starting to acquire their own transport and this accelerated the demise of the works' contract, and must have accelerated the increase in traffic congestion.

Despite the decline in traditional markets, Epsom Coaches were particularly well placed for the emerging tourist market in London as they had always maintained a modern fleet. They were ideally suited to the incoming tourist business and during the 1960's started working with Cosmos Tours and Friendship Tours. The Niemann family ran Friendship Tours from their offices in Ashtead, mainly offering package holidays to Holland. Roy Richmond even arranged a staff outing to Holland through Friendship Tours, chartering a Viscount aircraft for the day's outing, which included a visit to Maarse and Kroon, a Dutch coach operator.

By 1965 Epsom Coaches holiday programme was beginning to develop and included ten UK destinations. For £17, customers could take an 8-day centred holiday to the Isle of Wight staying at a B grade hotel, or for an extra £2 10s staying at an A grade hotel, the price even included gratuities for the hotel staff. At that time, the overseas part of the programme was organised in conjunction with Friendship Tours, and included several different tours to Holland, Belgium and Germany.

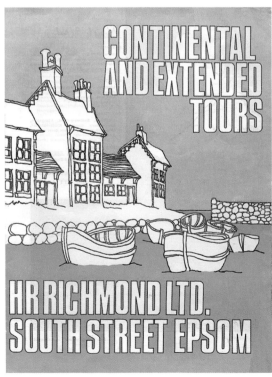

Cover from the 1967 Holiday brochure

The Company undertook regular runs from London to Manston Airport for Cosmos Tours and Friendship Tours. Passengers would fly to Rotterdam Airport by Invicta Airways using Douglas Skymaster and Viscount aircraft. Drivers would often stay overnight in lodgings near Manston, and carry out a return journey the next day. Manston Airport was an RAF base, and the atmosphere was informal, pilots would even use the same cafeteria as the passengers. It was said that passengers could overhear pilots discussing their lucky escapes, which must have done a lot for passenger confidence. Fortunately, Manston was also one of the safest airports to land, due to the emergency services provided by the RAF. At least one of the Invicta aircraft landed on a bed of foam following the suspected failure of its undercarriage. It is also said that a spare aircraft wheel was flown out to Holland strapped into one of the passenger seats. Coach drivers also had the opportunity of flying out to Holland, sometimes sitting in the cockpit with the crew when there weren't enough seats available. Air travel was much more basic in those days.

By 1967 the Company's holiday programme was growing and justified a separate brochure for the first time. It was printed in two colours and featured a holiday on each page, with brief description, route map, and photograph. The brochure included an 8-day tour to La Baule in Brittany which had not sold that well, so rather than cancel it, Roy decided to drive the coach, and take his family for a busman's holiday. Doris, Christopher, Andrew and Rosemary, Doris's father, and Roy's Aunt made up the numbers.

In July 1967 the Company suffered a major blow when a coach was involved in an accident near Dunkirk. The driver, Reg Burrows, and the party from the London Nautical School, had a narrow escape when a car came speeding from a side road into the path of the coach. The car became wedged under the front of the coach and caught light. Although the occupants of the car died in the incident, all of the coach passengers managed to get out in time, before the coach became engulfed in flames. The vehicle was destroyed along with the passengers' belongings.

Continental travel opened up a completely new market for the Company, with day excursions to Northern France and Belgium. Passengers without a passport could travel using an Identity Card issued by the Company. The card required a photograph, which the customer could provide, or alternatively, an instant Polaroid picture was taken at the time of booking. With the use of the Polaroid camera, late bookings were often accommodated by a snapshot taken at the picking up point in Waterloo Road, and the use of the Company's validation perforator. Customers found the experience amusing, and there were some light-hearted moments! Currency restrictions were also in force, and the amount of foreign exchange spent on each traveller had to be declared on a 'V' form, and entered in their passport.

In 1968, the decision was taken to open a travel agency opposite The Tower of London. The aim was to combine the shop with the coach station below, and act as a meeting place for early morning departures of Cosmos Tours and Friendship Tours. Peter Goldman

Tower Travel, Tower Hill, London

51

managed Tower Travel, and looked after the numerous passengers, whilst waiting for their connections by coach to Manston, Gatwick or Luton Airport. This venture was short lived as the demand for group transfers to airports diminished, and the shop lease was later sold.

During the late 1960's, the Labour Government wanted to nationalise road passenger transport and take over companies such as Epsom Coaches. Realising he could easily lose the coach business, Roy Richmond decided to expand the travel business that had been building up at the South Street booking office. The Company was also under pressure from the local council to move out of its South Street premises to make way for the Ashley Shopping Centre, and this would have meant losing its presence in the town. As a result, a suitable shop was found at 1 Ashley Road and in November 1968, Epsom Travel opened under the management of Colin Wyeth. A second shop, named Crescent Travel, was also opened near the Thorndike Theatre in Church Street, Leatherhead, under the management of Len Spencer.

Epsom Travel, 73 High Street, Epsom

Both travel offices thrived, and soon became IATA (International Air Transport Association) recognised, allowing them to issue airline tickets in their own right. The Epsom shop was very small, so rooms had to be rented across the road to cope with the administration. The business eventually outgrew itself, and was sold in favour of a larger rented unit at 73 High Street.

The Company opened a third travel agency in High Street, Banstead, and by this time they were all trading as Epsom Travel. Whilst all three shops had managers, Doris Richmond monitored the accounts for all three shops.

On 31st July 1969, the Company's founder, Roddy Richmond died at the age of 77. He had suffered from Parkinson's Disease and depression for some time, and spent the last year of his life in a nursing home in Leatherhead.

During the 1970's, the government introduced The Road Transport Industry Training Board (RTITB), which was financed by a 1% levy of the payroll, for operators with six coaches or more. The aim of the Board was to encourage companies to invest in training, and in planning their businesses. If companies could provide the Board with sufficient evidence to show they had training plans in place, they were entitled to a rebate of part, or all the monies paid. When the Board was originally set up, the officials had little idea of the industry they were about to advise, and Epsom Coaches were used in one of their fact-finding visits. The Board was administered by a quango based at luxurious offices in Wembley, and Roy Richmond acted as a representative for the coach industry in its early days. He soon discovered that the meetings, which were followed by lavish lunches, were a waste of his time, and he relinquished his position. The bureaucrats lived a different lifestyle, and it was generally felt that the levy did little to promote good business practice, and the government eventually closed it down.

In 1970, Roy's eldest son Christopher joined the Company, having gained an OND in business studies at South West London College. Christopher became the Tours Director and concentrated on building up the day tour and holiday business, producing most of the Company's brochures over the next 30 years. Up to this time, publicity had been fairly basic, mainly in the form of monochrome folded timetables and price lists. In the late 1970s, Christopher married Enid, and they have two children, James and Laura.

The first brochure Christopher produced was in 1970, the year that the Company celebrated its 50th year of operation. The brochure followed the existing format, monochrome insert with a three-colour cover in black, red, and gold to commemorate the Golden Anniversary. The brochure included an 8-day centred holiday in Cliftonville for £16, including dinner, bed and breakfast, a half-day excursion to Canterbury, a mystery tour, and tickets to two shows.

Following the spectacular failure of several large tour operators such as Court Line, the government came under pressure to provide legislation to safeguard money paid over to tour operators. New legislation was introduced that required all tour operators to provide a guarantee bond that would be used to refund passengers in the event of a company failure. Epsom Coaches have since had to provide renewable guarantee bonds each year to cover all its holiday passengers.

Christopher and Roy Richmond

Besides the licensing of drivers and routes, under the provisions of the 1930 Road Traffic Act, coaches require annual inspection by a Department of Transport inspector. In view of the size of the fleet, MOT testing has become an all-year round task for Epsom Coaches, and this excludes normal servicing and repairs. With the bodyshop and workshop facilities at Longmead, Epsom Coaches have the capability of undertaking most types of repair. Having said this, there is a growing tendency to outsource major repairs to specialist repairers or to buy factory exchange units. Exchange units may be more expensive, but they do help to keep downtime to a minimum.

Although the South Street garage had been extended several times, the fleet was expanding and more room was needed. The South Street premises were far from ideal and coaches had to reverse into the garage off the busy main road.

In 1970, the Longmead site became available and plans were drawn up for a purpose-built garage, which included workshops, paint shop, offices and flats on the one-acre site. The new building would provide the Company with first class facilities, amongst the best in the industry.

The garage officially started operation on 5th July 1971 and by that time the fleet consisted of 37 coaches ranging in size from 7 to 48 seats, and nine new vehicles were acquired that year. The fleet had a combined capacity of 1,429 seats, which was enough to carry 2 per cent of Epsom & Ewell's population.

Although telephone systems were improving, they were still fairly crude. In the South Street office, there had been a small manual switchboard; lines were identified by drop down tags denoting which

BPJ 555H – a 1970 Ford R192 with 41-seat Plaxton 'Panorama Elite' coachwork. Shown here at the 42nd Brighton Coach Rally. Driver Wally Priest

The Longmead garage under construction during 1970

ones were in use. Latterly, they used the more modern key and lamp system, and the move to Longmead saw the introduction of the first private telephone exchange, which enabled calls to easily be re-directed throughout the building.

Prior to the move to Longmead, the Company recruited Peter Gooch as their Traffic Manager. Peter had a great deal of experience in the coach business, having worked for Surrey Motors in Sutton for many years. Peter helped build up the coach hire business as well as being an important link with the incoming tour operators. He was also responsible for producing the first full colour brochures in 1973 and 1974. Peter stayed with the Company until his retirement in 1983.

In July 1971, Roy Richmond's other son, Andrew joined the business, initially as a holiday job until going to college, but then deciding to stay on and work for the Company. Andrew had an interest in the mechanical side of the business and looked after the running of the fleet for most of the seventies before moving to other areas of the business.

Longmead garage after completion

During the 1970's the Company started providing coaches for a number of London incoming tour operators such as Specialised Travel (SPECTRA) and Wilkintours, both of whom are customers to this day, Supertravel, IETO, Trans National, Gullivers Travel Agency, EC Travel, Maritz, to name but a few. Epsom Coaches carried out transfers to and from the airports, sightseeing days out, and extended tours of Britain and Ireland.

The largest job ever handled by the Company was for an American group called the Sweet Adelines, which is the female equivalent to the barbershop choir. Over 5,000 people were transported on a daily basis to and from the Royal Albert Hall, and on various days out. The dresses were such that each singer took up a double seat on the coach. There are numerous other nationalities that require group travel in London, but the American market has been the most constant, and helps keep the fleet busy throughout the year. The Japanese market was also extremely buoyant, until their economy deteriorated.

Following the growth in the incoming tourist industry, Roy Richmond became a regular visitor to London, taking him into the West End and The City. The visits were needed in order to negotiate coach hire tariffs and meeting clients from abroad. At one point, Roy would make a regular trip to an American operator in London, who paid weekly, as he went, for his coach hire requirements. Roy enjoyed his break from office routine.

It has always been important to allocate the right type of driver to the work, and many customers have their favourite driver, or drivers, that they request for their day out. Scheduling is one of the most difficult jobs to perform, especially in the peak of the season where demand for coaches can exceed the supply of vehicles and drivers. Over the years many people have taken on this challenging task, including Derek Jones, Bill Slocombe, Tony Newman, Ken Lifford, Steve Whiteway, Ron Thompson and Spencer Green, to name but a few.

Around this time most British coach designs had not addressed the problem of engine noise, which was particularly bad as the diesel engines were mounted at the front of the chassis, and protruded above floor level. Although AEC and Leyland were first with the concept, Bedford started to mount their engines underfloor and amidships with the introduction of the YRQ chassis in 1971, and shortly afterwards, the YRT (the 11 metre version). The new chassis soon gained popularity with operators who were looking for a reasonably priced vehicle with low noise levels and much improved passenger comfort. This configuration also allowed more room for the entrance steps as the engine was no longer in the way.

The mid-engined concept has remained the mainstay of the British coach market for many years although heavyweight chassis such as the Leyland Leopard, AEC Reliance and towards the end of the 1970's, the newly imported Volvo B58 chassis, gradually replaced the lightweight Bedfords.

WRU 869J – Bedford YRQ with 41-seat Plaxton Panorama Elite' coachwork.
This evhicle was usually driven by Alan Milner

The ordering and collection of new coaches has always been a pleasant experience, and salesmen from the manufacturers and agents visit the Company on a regular basis. Several of the coach dealers used to remind Roy of the character Arthur Daley, from the TV series 'Minder', but most were old friends, and very much part of the industry. In the very early days, Plaxtons of Scarborough gave every driver that collected a new coach from the factory a half crown, however, an owner might receive even better treatment and be invited to lunch with Mr Plaxton in the boardroom, who would take it upon himself to carve the roast joint.

During the 1950's, 60's and early 70's, the Epsom Coaches fleet was largely based on lightweight chassis, mainly Bedford and latterly Ford. This policy started to change in 1971 when the Company purchased a Seddon Pennine V8 with Plaxton Panorama Elite coachwork. The front-engined heavyweight vehicle had a distinctive roar, and was quite noisy compared to the mid-engined underfloor vehicles. The Seddon, and several other Ford coaches were eventually sold to Capricorn Travel of Ebury Bridge Road, London to undertake overland journeys from London via the Middle East to India, mainly carrying Australians.

After their life with the Company, coaches are sold on to other operators and many have ended up in far away places, such as Jamaica and India, but the majority pass to operators in the UK. On one occasion an Irish operator arrived early one evening to view a 29-seat coach and, being satisfied, produced the full payment, in cash, from his briefcase. Although many purchasers promise to re-spray the vehicles before putting them into service, this rarely happens, and the Company now makes a point of removing the name before letting a coach go.

This former Epsom Coaches Ford was destined for places further afield than leafy Surrey, namely, the Middle-East and India in the service of Capricorn Travel (See previous page)

In 1973, there was a severe shortage of fuel, and Epsom Coaches came to the rescue of many commuters by providing a free service between Epsom and Morden station. The Company was not allowed to charge for the service, as it had not been registered, however, it had spare capacity between regular contracts and gained positive publicity as a result. Up to four coaches a day were provided each way for the journey to Morden. The Company's fuel supplies were restricted to the previous year's levels, however this proved to be adequate throughout the crisis. Bus and coach operators were treated a great deal better than the private motorists who had to join the long queues at petrol stations. Fuel rationing books were issued to motorists, but they were never used.

The Epsom Coaches fleet expanded to cope with the influx of overseas tourists, and in 1973 the Company bought no less than eleven new coaches – 6 Bedford YRT's, 1 Bedford YRQ, 3 Leyland Leopard's and a Ford Transit minibus. Despite the high specification of the Epsom vehicles, coach design was still somewhat behind the times. Leyland were still producing chassis with an outside fuel tank guage up to 1980 – drivers on a long run would have to stop and carry out a visual inspection of the tank mounted guage in order to decide when refuelling was necessary. Although the Leyland Leopard was a very reliable chassis, its design had become dated. The dashboard layout, first used in the 1930's, was still in similar format in the early 1970's, the engine cooling system was inadequate and drivers would, on occasions, have to put the interior heaters on during the summer months to prevent the engine overheating. The Plaxton windscreen wipers had a separate electric motor for each side of the windscreen, which meant the two rarely went in unison, which was very distracting

This old Epsom coach was put to a more unusual use by Sanger's Circus

An interesting photograph taken in 2002 of Bedford TPE 550, once owned by Epsom Coaches, in its final resting place at the premises of Denyer Brothers, Standon Massey, Essex. An interesting comparison can be made by reference to a picture in original condition shown on page 35

KNR 328L – a 1973 Leyland Leopard with 53-seat Plaxton 'Panorama Elite' coachwork. Driver is Arthur Boswell

for the driver. Coach design has always lagged behind car design because it is difficult for the manufacturers to justify the investment in research and development, given the small numbers produced.

During the 1970's, one of the Company's coaches was stolen from the Victoria Embankment where it had been parked between journeys, a common practice when drivers are waiting in the West End. The driver phoned in with the news, and a replacement coach was immediately despatched to bring the party home. Having reported the matter to the Police, over a week went by without any news of its whereabouts. By this time, the Richmond's were wondering if they would ever get the coach back, and Andrew decided to have a look for himself. He drove to where the coach had been parked, and continued in an easterly direction, much to his surprise found the coach parked at the side of the road near Wapping, only yards from a Police Station! He reported the find to the Police, who took little interest, and then drove the vehicle back to the garage. There was another occasion when a coach was stolen from the Longmead garage, and dumped in Stoneleigh, after having damaged many parked cars along the way.

Chapter 5
THE MODERN ERA

By the late 1970's the touring programme had expanded, and now justified a full colour brochure. The destinations were also becoming more adventurous, and the 1976 programme offered a tour behind the Iron Curtain. The tour to Berlin took passengers through checkpoint Alpha, along the Corridor route to West Berlin, and visited East Berlin, after having first negotiated the famous border control, Checkpoint Charlie. In 1978, following the closure of Ben Stanley Limited of Walton-on-Thames, Epsom Coaches saw the potential for expansion, and introduced a Thameside Programme of day tours.

Over the years coaches have progressively increased in size. They originally had a maximum permitted length of 27 feet 6 inches, which was increased to 30 feet, then 10, 11 and now 12 metres. Currently there is pressure on the government to allow British coaches to match their European counterparts, where vehicles can be up to 15 metres in length. The width has also increased from 7' 6" to 2.5 metres, and now 2.55 metres. Epsom Coaches have always resisted the temptation to run double-deck vehicles as their service facilities are designed for single-deck vehicles only.

The Company's premises have been subject to continual development, although the basic structure remains. When the garage first opened, the longest coach was 11 metres long, and there were only four of them. With the introduction of 12 metre coaches in 1973, the width of the garage started to become a problem, and in 1979 the Company had to increase the length of the 34 vehicle parking bays to accommodate them. The site next door was also acquired and new facilities were built including a two-bay bodyshop, a larger drivers' rest room, new vehicle wash, an additional 13,500-gallon underground fuel tank as well as an extension to one side of the garage.

Ken LeLacheur driving the 1979 Leyland Leopard, HGN 307T.
This vehicle was fitted with Plaxton Supreme Mk4 coachwork

Epsom Coaches was one of the first private coach companies to introduce an automatic vehicle wash. The first machine, originally based at the South Street garage, was hailed as one of the most advanced vehicle washing systems in the world. The Ultrasonic vehicle washer utilised a frame that was lowered over the entire vehicle. Pressure jets located at regular intervals around the frame sprayed an acid based chemical at high pressure on to the coachwork to remove the dirt. The second pass of the frame sprayed an alkali to neutralise the chemicals, and finally the vehicles were given a rinse of water. Unfortunately, whilst the wash did not make contact with the vehicle, the chemical was not always neutralised, and corrosion resulted. There were other problems with the system that meant the frame could tilt and get stuck around the vehicle, if it wasn't positioned correctly. The machine was soon replaced by a conventional brush wash.

In 1980, two long standing competitors, Surrey Motors in Sutton, and RACS (Duvals) of Mitcham, both decided to close their coach operations. This was good news for Epsom Coaches who expanded their day trip and holiday touring programmes to cover some of the areas previously covered by the two companies; a separate Sutton area brochure was produced that year. The Company also employed two of the RACS drivers, Bill Bettison and Dave Gettings; Bill worked until his retirement, and Dave is still with the Company.

In 1985, Andrew Richmond married Lynn who had worked in the tours department since 1980. In 2000, Lynn completed a sponsored trek to Machu Picchu in aid of Barnados. Approximately forty fundraisers from throughout Britain took part in the trip, which took ten days to complete. After acclimatising to the high altitude (3,700 metres above sea level), the party set off along the Inca Trail. The party followed the Urumbamba River, ascended Dead Woman's Pass (4,200 metres), crossed Runkurakay Pass, and on to Intipunku (Gates of the Sun) where they experienced the sunrise overlooking the lost city of Machu Picchu, far below in the mist. After the descent to Machu Picchu, the group were shown round the vast historical site, before visiting Aguas Calientes, to enjoy a relaxing bath in the local hot springs. With the help of Steve Whiteway and the support of Epsom Coaches suppliers, Lynn raised over £3,300 for the charity.

In 1981 Epsom Coaches was privileged to carry the Australian Cricket Team on their three month UK tour. The driver, Peter Tribe, stayed with the team throughout their visit, and was so well thought of, that he was presented with a return ticket to Australia at the farewell party. The ticket allowed him to enjoy a five-week tour of Australia, which included the Tests between Australia and the West Indies in Adelaide, as well as visiting Melbourne, Sydney, Perth, and Brisbane, staying in the cricketers' homes in each town.

Seen here leaving Buckingham Palace is XGO 226W, a Bristol LHS driven by Paul Miller

63

Leyland Tiger advertisement showing Roy Richmond in the background

British heavyweight coach chassis designs were lagging behind their continental counterparts such as Volvo, so in 1981, Leyland introduced the Tiger, five of which were bought by Epsom Coaches over a two year period. The chassis was a complete redesign and incorporated air suspension, a new turbocharged engine, and even such refinements as a dashboard mounted fuel guage! Unfortunately, the design was such a radical change for Leyland that there were a lot of unproven new components and that made the vehicle unreliable, so by 1983 Epsom Coaches decided a change was needed. In that year, the first four Volvo B10Ms were introduced, two of which were destined for the French Riviera service that would require, and achieve, excellent levels of reliability. For coach use, the Company bought Volvo chassis exclusively for the next ten years.

The Company has always endorsed new technology, and were one of the first coach companies to use computers. In 1981, Andrew Richmond helped with the development of a system, which handled both the private hire and tour business. The Company invested a great deal in the system which was years ahead of the competition. It was hoped that some of the development costs would be recovered by selling the system on to other coach operators, however, this was not achieved. The programs had been specifically written to operate on a DEC computer system, and could not easily be transferred to the up and coming smaller, and lower cost, IBM systems. Nevertheless, the system remained the mainstay of the coach operation for well over ten years before adopting the new industry standard system.

Around this time, Roy Richmond had become very active in the coach operators trade association, the Bus and Coach Council (now named the Confederation of Passenger Transport), and he made frequent visits to their headquarters in London. He became Chairman of the London and Home Counties section of the association, and chaired many of the meetings for the region.

In 1982 Roy's daughter, Rosemary also joined the business. She assisted Christopher with the production of the Company's brochures, as well as putting together holidays for private groups, and helping with the busy tours department. She worked full-time for the Company until 1986, and is a member of the Board of Directors. Rosemary is married to Tim and has two children, Robert and Mark.

In 1982 Epsom Coaches started operating a daily commuter service to London from three areas, Dorking and Reigate, Great Bookham, and Tattenham Corner at a cost of £1.50 for the return fare, undercutting the rail fare by £1.20 per day. The Company saw the opportunity of making use of the large number of coaches that were running empty to and from London each day for the incoming tourist market. Although the services were well supported during the rail strikes that followed, they were eventually withdrawn due to competition from the faster, more frequent, rail service.

Amongst some of the more unusual stories, in May 1983 Epsom Coaches took 46 kidney patients from Dulwich Hospital for a day trip to Boulogne. Only 40 minutes before they were due to arrive back in Dover, they got an urgent message to say that a suitable donor had been found for one of the patients, a Sean Tompkins of West Croydon. The coach was given special clearance at customs and was driven immediately to a pre-arranged rendezvous with a police car, which took the patient the rest of the journey. Sean was in the operating theatre within an hour and seven minutes.

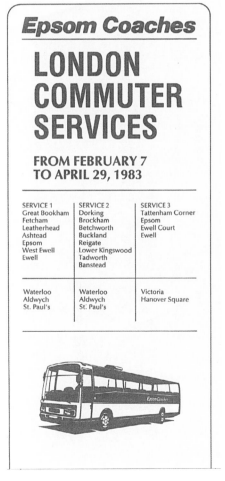

Epsom Coaches

LONDON COMMUTER SERVICES

FROM FEBRUARY 7 TO APRIL 29, 1983

SERVICE 1	SERVICE 2	SERVICE 3
Great Bookham	Dorking	Tattenham Corner
Fetcham	Brockham	Epsom
Leatherhead	Betchworth	Ewell Court
Ashtead	Buckland	Ewell
Epsom	Reigate	
West Ewell	Lower Kingswood	
Ewell	Tadworth	
	Banstead	
Waterloo	Waterloo	Victoria
Aldwych	Aldwych	Hanover Square
St. Paul's	St. Paul's	

The Company has held several Open Days over the years, and the one in 1983 was certainly one of the most successful. The event was opened by the Mayor of Epsom & Ewell Borough Council, Councillor Bill Carpenter, and attracted over 2,000 visitors. The event also incorporated a mini travel fair featuring more than 20 tourist attractions from around the South of England.

On display were two Volvo B10M coaches, one of which was destined for the London to Nice service, which started shortly afterwards. A couple of days before the event, Andrew Richmond visited Plaxtons of Scarborough with a colleague to collect the vehicles, only to find they were far from complete, even the entrance doors hadn't been fitted. After a long wait, Plaxtons put the two up at a local hotel for the night, and in the morning, after another long wait, were told that just one of the vehicles would be ready and the other one would be driven down overnight, ready for the Open Day.

Also on display, and in contrast to the two new vehicles, was a 33 seat 1951 Bedford coach that had originally belonged to Epsom Coaches. A local policeman, Geoff Heels, spotted the old coach with a 'For Sale' sign on the forecourt of a petrol station, whilst on holiday with his family in Devon. He paid £150 for it, but the vehicle had to undergo complete restoration.

NGT 1Y – Volvo B10M with 44-seat Plaxton Paramount 3500 bodywork, destined for the Riviera Express Service

1983 Open Day – Geoff Heels, Ernie Warwick (retired coach driver) and Roy Richmond by PPH 698, a 1951 33-seat Bedford SBG with Duple Vista bodywork

Also on display was an unusual six-wheeled mini-moke, which had been built by Andrew Richmond and Mick Sayers, the Bodyshop Foreman. The six-wheeler was used for many years as a general runabout for the Company, before being replaced by something a little more practical.

A good friend of Roy's, Francis Flin, approached the Company towards the end of 1982 with the idea of operating a luxury coach service from Victoria Coach Station through to the French Riviera. The service, unlike the competition, would travel by daytime only, and have a proper overnight stop en route at a hotel in Auxerre.

The new Riviera Express service suffered from the age-old problem of licensing,

Mick Sayers and Andrew Richmond by the six-wheel mini pick-up

however, this time it involved the French authorities. European legislation has since been relaxed, but the opposition at that time required a meeting with the French Ministry of Transport in Paris, who proved to be very uncooperative and tried to block the application. Epsom Coaches eventually met all the obligations necessary under European law, and agreed to share the service with a French partner Cars Phoceen of Nice. Even after the licence was granted, the French gendarmerie looked for rewards and on one occasion stopped the coach en route and fined the driver £80, alleging that his documents were not in order, which was far from the truth. The driver had to pay the money – it was a question of paying up or delaying the sevice.

The Riviera Express operated with two Volvo B10M Plaxton Paramounts, which had been fitted with air-conditioning, toilet, a water boiler for drinks, refrigerator, video, underfloor driver's bunk, and 44 luxury reclining seats. One of the passengers on the inaugural service was Carol Thatcher, daughter of the Prime Minister, who wrote an article for one of the national newspapers.

In April 1984 the Company ran a rather unusual day trip, entitled the 'April Fool's Tour' which was a mystery tour that included a visit to a folly and a funfair on, appropriately enough, April 1st. For the trip, the drivers were dressed up as jesters, and each passenger was given an April Fool's Pack containing a hot cross bun, a funny hat and a signed certificate to show they were fool enough to take part.

While convalescing from a minor operation in August 1986, Roy Richmond decided he would take advantage of the impending deregulation of local bus services. Surrey County Council were inviting tenders for some local routes, and the Company was also looking at starting a new commercial route that linked Epsom and Tolworth, serving the Watersedge and Longmead Estates en route (Route 5).

Deregulation of local bus services came at a good time for the Company as the coach hire business had been severely affected by the terrorist activities of Colonel Gadaffi, and the incoming tourists, especially Americans, were not visiting Britain. This left the Company with a surplus of coaches and drivers.

On the first day of deregulation, 26th October 1986, Epsom Buses started operating its new commercial route number 5. Shortly afterwards, the Company

Leyland Tiger coach AGJ 344W with Plaxton Supreme body, in the deep mid-winters snow, whilst working on the 598 bus service

learnt that they had been successful in tendering for Surrey County Council bus routes 598 and 516. The 598 ran between Epsom and Croydon via Banstead, and the 516 operated between Box Hill and Leatherhead via Headley.

Although deregulation had taken place, routes still needed to be registered giving 42 days notice to the Traffic Commissioners before starting, or making any changes. The only exception to this was for the London area, where London Buses maintain control of all services and licences.

At the start, Epsom Buses used older coaches on its newly gained routes, mainly 12 metre Leyland Leopards with Plaxton Supreme coachwork, and Mercedes-Benz L608D with Plaxton Mini Supreme coachwork for the Box Hill service. Whilst the coach chassis were very capable of providing reliable service, the coach bodies were unsuitable for the type of work, having a narrow

D202 PGJ, a Mercedes-Benz L608D with Plaxton Mini-Supreme body for 20 passengers

entrance door, tinted double glazed side windows, reclining seats, as well as being far longer and less manoeuvrable than conventional buses. It therefore became clear that purpose built vehicles were required, and in 1987 the Company purchased five new Bedford YMT buses with Plaxton Derwent bodywork.

Up to deregulation, the major bus companies had had it all their own way, and levels of service were quite often poor. The companies

Bedford YMT bus, D603 RGJ, with Plaxton Derwent bodywork

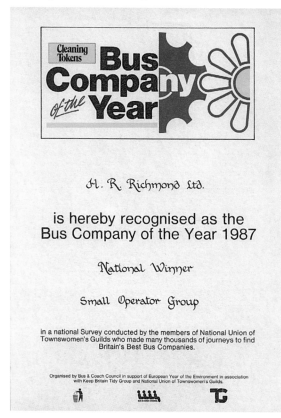

were also under the stranglehold of the unions, and the closed shop principle reigned, so it was difficult for them to introduce more efficient working practices. Competition was therefore very unwelcome by those working for these companies, and Epsom Buses drivers experienced a spell of antagonism as a result. For a short period, drivers were deliberately blocked in at bus stops to prevent them carrying on their journeys, and there was an unusually high spate of damage caused to the Epsom Buses vehicles by other companies buses, usually whilst they were stationary waiting at bus stops.

The quality and positive attitude of the Epsom drivers soon made an impact on the industry, and the Company was judged UK Bus Company of the Year in 1987 (Small Operator Group), just a year after

Mercedes-Benz Model L709D midibus, F208 GGH,
picking up-customers on service 5 to Epsom. Driver Keith Garner

the services began. The Bus and Coach Council had asked Townswomen's Guilds throughout the country to complete mystery traveller reports, and Epsom Buses were judged the best for the size of business. The Company has continued to offer standards to which most companies aspire, and has won many other awards. Roy Richmond was interviewed on Radio 4 regarding his Company's achievements.

The introduction of bus services brought new challenges for the Company - timetables, fare tables, duty rosters, ticket machines and bus stops all had to be put in

K321 GEW, one of the earlier Darts with Marshall 40-seat bus body
seen here in Croydon on Service 166. It is in a later Quality Line livery

place within a six week timescale, before the new services could start. They purchased a number of second-hand Setright ticket machines that had already seen a great deal of service, having been converted from pounds, shillings and pence. They were eventually replaced by electronic ticketing equipment after eight years in service. The electronic machines have the advantage of storing all the Company's fare chart information, as well as infomation on every ticket sold. The data is downloaded from the drivers' modules at the end of a day, and the system provides full details of ticket transactions by date, route, and driver. The ticket information for the London Buses services is automatically downloaded to London Buses by modem each day.

Operating cross boundary routes can produce illogical fares between London and its surroundings, and the Company is often blamed for the discrepancies that arise. All bus services are subsidised, and most, if not all, services would disappear if these subsidies were withdrawn. A large section of the community do not have access to, or are unable to run their own transport, and these needs have to be met by the local authorities and the government. All services receive a rebate of most of the fuel tax paid, and other income derives from local authorities route subsidies, allowance for the acceptance of school and OAP passes, receipt of fares, and specific payments for the provision of services where there would otherwise be none. The system for financing bus services in Surrey is somewhat complex, whereas tendered services in London are provided on a straightforward sum for operating the service, and all fares are collected and returned to the authority.

During the early eighties, a local engineer, Barry Wohlman, constructed an unusual motorised replica of one of the Epsom Coaches. The model, which was based on a Volvo B10M chassis with Plaxton Paramount coachwork, had a motorbike engine, and gave rides for children at local events to raise money for the Queen Mary's Hospital in Carshalton.

Another model of an Epsom Coach was produced by Corgi Classics Limited of Leicester. The 1/76th scale model of the Dennis Javelin coach with Plaxton Premiere coachwork was based on an actual coach registration number M793 LPH. The model even displayed the Coach Operator of the Year 1996/7 decals that were taken from the original.

The motorised replica of an Epsom Coaches vehicle, built by Barry Wohlman

On 29th April 1988, Roy Richmond received a letter from the Principal Private Secretary of the Prime Minister to inform him that his name had been put

forward recommending that he be appointed a Member of the Order of the British Empire (MBE). The award was given for his services to the passenger transport industry and the Investiture took place on Wednesday, 30th November 1988 at Buckingham Palace.

1/76th scale diecast model of an Epsom Coaches Dennis Javelin/Plaxton Premiere, produced by Corgi

In 1990 the family agreed to some changes to the board of Directors. Roy Richmond became Chairman, and Andrew Richmond was appointed Managing Director. The other Directors were Doris Richmond as Company Secretary, Christopher Richmond as Tours Director, and Rosemary Lever.

Roy and Christopher Richmond at Buckingham Palace

Roy Richmond has always taken a keen interest in local affairs. He has been a member of the Epsom Rotary Club since 1959, having taken his turn at the Presidency, is a member of PROBUS, and is involved in various charitable works within the Borough. He is also a long-standing member of the Epsom Chamber of Commerce, and became their youngest President in 1958, and had a further term as President during 1997 and 1998. Amongst his other interests, Roy also became President of the Epsom & Ewell Silver Band, and latterly helped form the Butterfly Appeal with the help of his second wife, Nancy. It was Roy's involvement in the local community that gave rise to him becoming an Honorary Freeman of the Borough of Epsom & Ewell in 1991.

The Directors and Managers of H R Richmond Limited celebrate the 70th anniversary of the business. Left to right: Chris Foale, Alistair Scott, Andy Gallagher, Christopher Richmond, Roy Richmond, Andrew Richmond, Steve Whiteway, David Blackmore, Brian Mutter

EPSOM & EWELL
BOROUGH COUNCIL

Conferment of the Title

of

Honorary Alderman of the Borough

on

Former Councillor Harold Rhead Newton, MBE

and

Honorary Freeman of the Borough

on

Roydon Bircham Richmond, MBE

at 1930 hours on

Wednesday 27 November 1991

at the

Town Hall, The Parade, Epsom

The recession in the early 1990's affected Epsom Coaches business, and as a result, the coach replacement programme was cut back. The Company had been buying Volvo B10M vehicles with Van Hool coachwork between 1988 and 1993, however, the price of imported coaches had risen, and a suitable alternative needed to be found. One of the vehicles they had considered buying for some time was the British built Dennis Javelin, and a number of demonstration vehicles had been assessed. The Company also had experience of the Dennis product on the bus side of the business, and had operated the first in a long line of Dennis Darts. They had been impressed with the reliability and

Volvo B10M, H532 WGH, with Van Hool Alizee coachwork.

good fuel economy. The Javelin chassis was not only a British product, but also offered better fuel consumption than the Volvo, and more usable luggage space. As a result, a large number of Dennis Javelins were purchased between 1994 and 1999 and many are still in service at the time of writing.

The purchase of new coaches has always placed a heavy financial burden on the Company, in common with the rest of the industry. The coach business is very seasonal, profitable during the summer months, and incurring losses throughout the winter months. The Company usually sells off its old coaches at the end of each season and takes on new vehicles in time for the following year. The requirements for the bus fleet are mainly geared to the success or failure when

Four Dennis Javelins with Plaxton Premiere 320 coachwork outside the Dennis factory at Guildford

tendering for routes. The budget for new buses and coaches is now well in excess of one million pounds per annum. Back in 1946 a 29-seater coach cost in the region of £1,600, but today, the equivalent size coach would cost approximately £95,000, and a 49-seat coach costs in the region of £200,000. Buses cost between £75,000 and £100,000 depending on the size and specification.

Epsom Coaches have always tried to take the lead and became the first coach company in the country to fit seat belts as standard across its fleet. They were also one of the first companies to fit air-conditioning and double-glazing as standard equipment, making winter travel far more pleasant by keeping the windows mist-free, and improving passenger comfort. Their touring fleet also includes the fitment of toilet/washrooms, and tea/coffee making facilities. These vehicles are largely used for the Epsom Holidays touring programme, although they are also available for general hire.

Following the government's requirement for tour operators to provide security bonds to guarantee passengers' money, operators that owned and operated their own vehicles were put at a financial disadvantage, so much so that H R Richmond Limited took the opportunity to set up two subsidiary companies in September 1992. The travel agency business then traded as Epsom Travel Limited, and the day tour and holiday operation traded as Epsom Tours Limited.

In 1995, two non-family Directors were appointed to the board of Directors. Steve Whiteway was appointed Operations Director, and Andy Gallagher as Finance Director. Steve had worked with the Company since joining as a coach driver in 1980. His potential was recognised, and he soon joined the office team, becoming an Operations Controller. He then progressed to the coach hire section, before becoming Commercial Director, responsible for the day to day operation of the coach and bus fleet. Andy Gallagher looked after financial matters until he left the Company in 1999.

Over recent years, the Company has gained several awards in recognition of the quality of its operation. The first of these was in 1996 when it received an Energy Efficiency award at the Surrey Business Awards ceremony. Epsom Coaches were chosen because of the measures it had taken to use fuel more efficiently, and reduce other forms of energy by good housekeeping.

The Company has also achieved successive triumphs at the Bus and Coach Awards. At the 1996/97 Coach and Bus Week Awards in Bournemouth, Epsom Coaches ran away with most of the awards having won the Overall Coach Operator of the Year, Coach Operator of the Year (16-39 vehicles), Coach Manager of the Year – Steve Whiteway, Fleet Livery of the Year and the Safety Award.

In November 1997, Epsom Buses came to an agreement with London General to take over the operation of the S1 and 413 bus routes, and bought eleven used Optare Metrorider buses from them to operate the routes. It soon became clear that the vehicles would need to be replaced in order to improve reliability, so in

Steve Whiteway at the Surrey Business Awards (Presenter Anna Ford on the right)

*The Epsom Coaches Team with Tom O'Connor
at the 1996/97 Coach and Bus Week Awards,after having won five awards*

1999 the Company came to an agreement with London Buses to invest in eleven new Dennis Mini Pointer Darts.

With the introduction of the new vehicles on these routes, the opportunity was taken to re-launch the bus division under a new name to reflect the Company's aims. Whilst still retaining Epsom Buses, the name Quality Line was added, and a QL symbol introduced. The

H683 YGO, a former London General *Optare Metrorider, during respray to Epsom Coaches livery*

latest vehicles have dropped the name Epsom Buses altogether and operate under the Quality Line banner. Buses allocated to the London bus routes are now painted in the traditional London Buses red livery.

The Company has set new standards for its bus operation and introduced many new initiatives in order to improve customer satisfaction. Large clocks, accurately tuned to the Rugby time signal were fitted to buses to improve punctuality. Drivers' air conditioning units were installed to improve working conditions, public address to

S454 LGN in advertising livery but also displaying the 'QL' Quality Line logo

announce stops and double glazing to improve customer comfort. Epsom Buses also helped London Buses trial the use of background music on one of its buses. Tests were carried out to see whether passengers were happier with or without the music, and to see whether music could reduce the levels of graffiti and vandalism.

The Company continues to review and develop all sides of the business. On the bus side, routes that had been taken on commercially such as the K9/K10, and the 166, had become uneconomic over the years due to increased operating costs, and notice was eventually given which resulted in the routes going out to tender. The Company was successful in retaining the K9/K10, but lost the 166 to Arriva, who were already undertaking part of the route. The E5, originally developed by the Company, still maintains its commercial status, despite competition from other services.

Although the retail travel businesses had been successful in their early years, the business had started to decline as more travel shops came into the towns and competition from the multiple agencies became fiercer. The larger travel companies were able to justify national advertising campaigns, promoting discounts off holidays. In reality, these offers meant that customers would normally be offered a discount, but would end up having to take expensive travel insurance as part of the deal, however the power of advertising was very strong. The directors also felt the Company should

Route S5, now operated within London Buses Route 463.

In London red. Mini-Pointer Dart, SD 13 (S459 LGN), with Plaxton 29-seat bodywork heading for Morden Station on the S4

concentrate on its core business and specialise in what it did best. The travel agencies were sold over a number of years; the Leatherhead branch to Sun City Travel, the Banstead branch to Ashtead Travel, and the Epsom branch to Grantfern Limited under the Epsom Worldchoice banner in October 1999.

In the same year that Epsom Travel was sold, Christopher Richmond took the decision to leave the Company, and he and his wife Enid achieved their ambition of setting up an hotel in the West Country. The tour operation is now managed by Alistair Scott, who has worked with the Company since 1988, and is now responsible for publishing the day tour and holiday programmes. The Company continues to offer a wide range of high quality holidays and has seen steady growth with many new destinations on offer.

The continued excellence of its operation was recognised in the 1999 Bus Industry Awards. The Company won the Judges' Special Award in the Bus Operator of the Year category as well as being Highly Commended in the Sema Group Innovation Award. In the same year, the coach operation was runner up in the Coach Operator of the Year Award (17-40 vehicles) at the Coach and Bus Week Awards.

Further success came the following year when the Company's bus operation was singled out for inclusion in the Spiral of Achievement at the Millennium Dome in Greenwich. The Quality Line operation was judged to be worthy of Millennium Product status, standing alongside the most innovative and best of British companies represented at the Dome. The same year at the 2000 Coach and Bus Week Awards,

The appropriately registered A9 HRR, in metallic paintwork to celebrate the 80th Anniversary

Epsom Coaches became finalists in the Corporate Identity of the Year Award, winner of the Day Excursion programme of the Year Award, Highly Commended in the Best British Coach Operator Award, and Winner of the Coach Operator of the Year Award (17-40 vehicles).

In the 2001 Coach and Bus Week Awards, Epsom Coaches won a silver award in the Day Excursion Programme of the Year category, a gold award in the Coach Operator of the Year (17-40 vehicles) category, and Spencer Green, the Company's Operation Manager, won a bronze award in the Coach Manager of the Year category.

Roy and Andrew Richmond with the 2001 Coach Operator of the Year Award

Chapter 6
TODAY'S OPERATIONS

Epsom Coaches operation is probably the best equipped organisation of its kind in this country. This chapter will give a brief outline of the current operation and explain the extent to which the Company goes in order to achieve customer satisfaction.

One of the essentials for any modern business is proper training. The Company has had its own PSV driving school for well over thirty years and spends a great deal of time and effort to ensure its staff fully understand all aspects of their jobs. Proper training requires the correct facilities, and these were upgraded in 2001 with the latest computerised audio visual equipment. Training sessions are regularly held, covering all aspects of employment from induction through to retirement and pensions advice.

The Company's offices have been subject to continual development over the years, and provide excellent working conditions. The networked computer system

The Company's training facilities

Part of the coach hire and operations office

provides users with the ability to access information throughout the building, and many of the programs are linked in order to save time, and improve efficiency. The system has normal word processing, desktop publishing, accounting, payroll and spreadsheet functions, but can also carry out specialist tasks such as coach hire costing, providing road mapping information throughout the world, record passenger and coach bookings, store bus ticket information and monitor vehicle fuel. The system is also connected to the internet, and the Company's websites (epsomcoaches.com & epsomholidays.com) can be maintained remotely from their offices. There is even a computer terminal in the drivers' rest room to give access to the internet.

Inevitably, with a fleet of eighty vehicles to look after, accident damage will occur from time to time. To cope with such situations, the Company has two repair and spray shops that are equipped to handle most eventualities. Where possible, downtime is reduced by spraying standard panels in the Company's colours, ready for fitting to the vehicle when it is taken out of service. There are two full-time members of staff dedicated to the smart appearance of the fleet.

The fleet also requires regular servicing and repairs, which are undertaken in the

A section of the workshop facilities

four bay workshop. Regular safety inspections are carried out every four weeks for buses, and six weeks for coaches. On top of this, vehicles have to be serviced according to the manufacturers' recommendations, and require an extensive annual MOT test. The facilities at Longmead include a rolling road brake tester which provides an accurate wheel by wheel assessment of the braking efficiency. Modern vehicles also make use of computers and faults can be diagnosed using a laptop computer. The service team regularly attend manufacturers' training courses to keep up to date with the latest developments.

Regardless of how modern the coach, they are only as good as the people who drive them. Few people realise just how much responsibility a coach driver has; not only is he responsible for the life of his passengers, he also has under his control a vehicle that may be valued at up to £200,000. The driver is, therefore, a vital part of the work force and has to be a good ambassador for the Company.

Most of Epsom Coaches driving team are trained from scratch in the Company's own driving school, to attain the necessary vocational qualification required to drive these modern and sophisticated machines. Regardless of experience, every driver is regularly assessed and is provided with regular training from the Training Manager in order to to maintain his or her status as a modern day 'knight of the road'.

In order to ensure a team of well trained driving staff, Epsom Coaches has a dedicated training vehicle. Dennis Dart bus K321 GEW was converted for the task and is also shown on page 71 when still in service

The coach fleet is one of the largest and most modern in the area. It consists of 34 vehicles varying in size from 7 seat minibuses through to 53 seat coaches. All vehicles are air-conditioned which is something that few other companies can boast. A modern fleet also means that Epsom Coaches run one of the safest fleets in the country. All coaches have anti-lock braking systems, factory fitted seat belts, and comply to the latest R66 European rollover safety standard. Positioned at the top end of the coach market, it firmly believes in offering its customers the best. The aim is to provide safe, comfortable, modern coaches that are well maintained and driven by skilled, friendly, helpful and knowledgeable drivers.

Volkswagen Caravelle 7-seat minibus, one of nine similar vehicles used on a dedicated contract

For the 2002 coaching season, the Company has invested in two new German

Covers of the 2002 Day, Coach & Air Tour brochures, emphasising the worldwide scope of the Company's present day operations

manufactured Setra coaches which are considered to be the very best available in Europe. In a new development, the Company has also recently purchased a fleet of nine new personnel carriers to provide staff transport for a locally based pharmaceutical company.

Amongst the varied work, Epsom Coaches supply coaches to the Corporation of London to transfer VIP's to and from the Guildhall or Mansion House for State Visits and Special Occasions. During one of these visits, Margaret Thatcher and Lord Hailsham travelled by Epsom Coaches. Other regular hirers include Sotheby's and the Royal Ballet School.

Epsom Holidays currently look after over 11,000 passengers on the day tour programme, and over 5,000 passengers per annum on its holiday programme. Epsom Holidays Travel Club was introduced in 2000, and now has over 1,500 members. Club members receive the benefits of newsletters, special offers and can take part in special club outings.

V511 MGO, a 27-seat Iveco 'Indcar Maxim' coach, introduced in 2000

A line of Epsom Coaches inside the garage at Longmead

Alexander bodied SLF Dart, fleet number SD 34, passing through the wash at Longmead. Environmentalists will be pleased to learn that this particular installation recycles up to ninety per cent of the water used

Quality Line, the Company's bus division, now operate a fleet of over 40 buses on local routes within Surrey and South London. Eight new vehicles joined the fleet at the beginning of 2002, to operate on the renewed contract to run the S1 service for London Buses. The latest vehicles have speed restrictors for safety and are equipped with eight video surveillance cameras in order to reduce the problem of vandalism and graffiti. This side of the business has seen substantial growth,

Table—showing Epsom Buses Quality Line Services (October 2002)			
Route **From**	**Via**	**To**	**Operated for**
E5 Langley Vale/Wells Estate	Epsom	Watersedge	Commercial
K9 Epsom	Manor Park	Kingston	Surrey County Council
K10 Epsom Hospital	Worcester Park	Kingston	Surrey County Council
E9 Epsom	Manor Park	Clarendon Park	Surrey County Council
408 Sutton	Epsom	Cobham, Sainsburys	Surrey County Council
S1 Mitcham	Sutton	Banstead	London Buses
S3 Worcester Park	Sutton	Royal Marsden Hospital	London Buses
S4 Morden	Sutton	Roundshaw	London Buses
404 Coulsdon	Old Coulsdon	Caterham-on-the-Hill	London Buses
463 Mitcham	Wallington	Coulsdon	London Buses

having doubled the fleet strength in just five years. The future also looks promising as government policy is aimed at reducing car usage by investing in better, more reliable public transport services.

Although the business has grown tremendously over the years, it still retains the family atmosphere. The staff recently voted by a significant majority to reject union recognition, and opted to retain the present open door management policy. Whilst the business has increased in size, it still retains the personal touch, and it is interesting to note that traditions such as Roy Richmond providing the staff with hot cross buns at Easter, and mince pies at Christmas, continue to this day. For the future, the Company will continue to develop by having a clear set of goals, and by not being afraid to adapt to new challenges. By following these principles it is certain to maintain a healthy business for many years to come.

BX02 CMU, one of the Company's Setra 48-seat touring coaches introduced for the 2002 season

Chapter 7

GENERAL RECOLLECTIONS
AND CHARACTERS

In September 1995, Roy and Andrew Richmond visited one of the first charabanc drivers, Bill Tinker MBE, who, at the age of 91, recalled with great clarity, some of his experiences whilst driving for the family firm from November 1921 to January 1923.

Bill left school and went to work at the age of 12, after losing both of his parents. He first joined W R Page (Motor Engineers) and completed a three-year apprenticeship with them before starting work for Bob Sadler in Ewell. Although Mr. Sadler was a butcher by trade, Bill drove a hire car belonging to him. One day he came to Bill and asked him if he wanted to do a job for a friend of his.

Mr Sadler took Bill to Epsom and introduced him to Mr Richmond, who had just taken delivery of a new Model T Ford charabanc and was looking for a driver to take a party to Sandown Racecourse that day. Bill's only previous knowledge of charabancs was limited to travelling on an away fixture for Epsom Wednesday Football Club to Dorking. On that occasion, he remembered arriving at the garage in Epsom High Street and boarding an open vehicle by means of a ladder, and sitting on forms along either side of the body.

Bill was only 16 (there was no age limit for driving charabancs) when he carried out his first job to Sandown. After that, he did occasional runs for Mr Richmond including one taking the Warwick family from Epsom Common to Brasted in Kent to go hop picking. Another day he took a doctor, his wife, two children, nanny, dog and luggage to their holiday home in Peacehaven and collected them a fortnight later. He also recalled taking a family from West Hill down to Ockley to attend a wedding. Although he only undertook occasional work for Richmond's during the summer of 1921, he became a full-time driver in November of that year, when Mr Sadler's business failed.

On one occasion, Bill recalled there were four charabancs employed to take servicemen to a titled Lady's home somewhere in the Staines area. The garden led down to the River Thames and there were sandwiches and cakes spread out on tables. When the time came for tea, Bill approached the table and the Lady said to him "what are you doing here, you're not a wounded soldier". When Mr Richmond explained that Bill was one of the charabanc drivers, she said. "What, a charabanc driver? He's only a boy!" Despite this, he did get his tea.

Bill recalled an incident that occurred whilst parked at Bognor one wet day. He was chatting to a couple of other drivers who had joined him in his charabanc. Whilst talking he noticed the canvas hood had billowed with water, and without thinking pushed it up to cascade the contents over the side, not realising there was a man passing by – who got the lot! One of the other drivers, George Ewer (founder of Grey-Green Coaches, part of the present day Arriva Group), lifted the side curtain and started laughing when he saw what had happened. Bill also lifted the side canvas, but unfortunately received a black eye from the man. Mr Richmond reminded Bill of the incident over the following years, much to everyone's amusement.

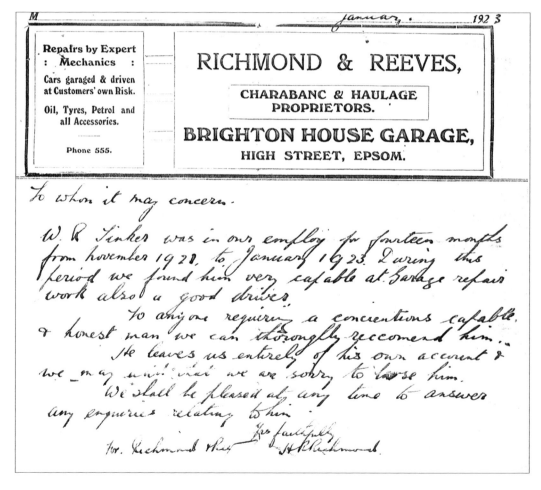

Bill Tinker's reference from H R Richmond

Bill Tinker cutting the ribbon to open the 2000 Open Day
Left to right - Steve Whiteway, Cyril Pawsey, Bill Tinker,
Phil Allport (in 1950's uniform), Andrew Richmond

In the year 2000, the Richmond's asked Bill if he would like to cut the ribbon to mark the start of the Open Day to commemorate the Company's 80th anniversary. Bill, then aged 96, kindly agreed, and spent several hours discussing old times and viewing the historic exhibits. He was also photographed with a Model T Ford charabanc similar to the one he drove, and was heard to comment that it had been one of the best days of his life. Sadly, Bill Tinker died the following year on 31st August.

There have been a number of long serving members of staff throughout the years, and notably, Albert Wall and Ernie Warwick drove coaches and horseboxes for the company from the early 1920's until the outbreak of war. After carrying out their national service, the two continued as coach drivers, right through to the time the business transferred to Longmead in 1971.

Between the wars, the company employed two mechanics, one by the name of George Allen, and the other, who was deaf and dumb, by the name of Dennis Barnes. Roddy Richmond soon learnt to communicate by the use of sign language.

In the early days, the two Albion coaches were driven by Hugh Perry and Bill Cottee, the Gilford by Arthur Deadmarsh, and the Bedfords by Ernie Shrub, Reg Beams and his nephew Jack, until the war.

Hugh Perry, Ernie Shrubb, Ernie Warwick and Albert Wall drove the first 29-seat coaches from 1946, and Bob Woods drove the 32-seat Albion with tender loving care until its eventual replacement following the war, avoiding Reigate Hill at all costs.

As the size of the fleet increased after the war, more drivers were taken on, including two Canadians, Charlie Cross and Bill Resoun, who stayed in England after the war finished. Charlie Cross drove for the company between 1950 and 1987.

Albert Wall on a visit to a Longmead Open Day during his retirement

Driver Arthur Deadmarsh by the Gilford coach PL 503 circa 1932

It is difficult to recollect the names of the early horsebox drivers, with the exception of Bill Beeching who worked for the company before and after the war. The post war horsebox drivers included George Rice, Freddie Bale, Mick Dillon, Fred Landsley and Ted Penfold. Roy Richmond would often have to take their orders out to their homes the evening before the job, and provide them with adequate petrol coupons, and subsistence in cases where they were staying away for the night.

People often leave their property on coaches, and quite often fail to claim their articles, some of which can be amusing. One girl left her guitar on the coach several weeks in succession - presumably she was trying to tell her parents something about the lessons for which they had presumably paid! An athletics club managed to leave a pole vault in the side locker of one of the coaches - not an easy item to mislay!

Roddy Richmond used to tell of a coach operator in Merton whose front door bell rang one night and the caller asked if she could get into the coach garage to collect her baby who was fast asleep on the back seat of the coach. The ladies night out had been so good; the mother had departed from the coach, leaving her baby behind.

Passengers do occasionally get lost when visiting another town or city. It is very frustrating for both the driver and the other passengers, leaving everyone in doubt as to whether that person is sick, or involved in an accident. One of the more vague passengers did this on a regular basis and eventually had to be banned from travelling – he was last seen in the Bruges area! When this happens, the driver has to report the missing person to the local police, leave reasonable time, and then move on.

One day Roy Richmond saw a coach passing the window of the South Street office, on its way to its next job. He happened to see a boy sitting on the back seat of the coach and realised nobody should be on board. With quick thinking, he got into his car and drove to Woodcote Hurst where the next job started. He arrived to find that the driver had just discovered the boy on the back seat - he had apparently been afraid of the teacher and decided to stay on the coach. Roy took the boy back to school.

The patients from the local mental hospitals were allowed out during the day and many could be trusted, but were unsuitable for regular work. Henry, a one-armed patient from a local hospital would sweep the yard, however he would often disappear leaving a pile of rubbish behind.

Another patient, George, thought he was being helpful by stopping the traffic outside the South Street garage, every time a coach needed to reverse in, however he was in many ways more of a hindrance than a help. He had been told not to do this on several occasions as his good intentions could easily have come to grief. One evening when Roy Richmond pulled up outside the garage, George immediately ran into the middle of the road to stop the traffic, but on this occasion Roy decided to drive the coach off, leaving him standing in the middle of the road.

Another patient caused amusement one lunchtime. Some of the office staff were on their way into the town centre when they spotted a naked lady walking along Waterloo Road – they couldn't believe their eyes.

Originally the business was located in the town and the fellow tradesmen were very friendly towards each other and helped to make Epsom a pleasant town in which to work. Roddy Richmond had established close relationships with other businessmen in the High Street and South Street. Rather than boil a kettle, Roy and his father would cross the road to the Rendezvous Café in South Street for a morning cup of tea.

In the early seventies, Epsom Coaches took on a driver, Malcolm Dobson, who had a liking for the 1950's. Although smartly dressed in the Company's uniform, he would don fluorescent pink or mauve socks beneath. At the Company social events, he went the whole hog and wore the full teddy boy outfit.

On one occasion Epsom Coaches employed a driver that had completed his army service, having gained his PSV Driving Licence before joining civilian life. His experience with the Company started off very well and the customers made glowing remarks about him. He reported for standby duty one day, and without warning disappeared with the Company's Ford Escort which incidentally also had a bag containing Steve Whiteway's washing in it. The next day, a hotel phoned the office to say that one of Epsom Coaches' drivers had stayed the night and left without paying the bill. Approximately four months went by before the Police phoned to say they had recovered the van in Wales with approximately 4,000 additional miles on the clock. Unfortunately Steve Whiteway's underwear was never recovered.

In the early days of the bus services, Epsom Buses employed a driver by the name of Robert Cullen. Robert was a real character and very kind to everyone. His generosity extended to buying cakes and sweets for his passengers, which could mean an unscheduled stop at Allen's Cake Shop in Upper High Street, or at the tea stall on Headley Heath. He would also buy gifts for the girls in the office.

The Company has also had its connections with various celebrities over the years. Coaches have been supplied to Elton John for a pub-crawl with some of his friends; Dick Emery hired a coach for an evening trip to London; Jimmy Edwards called upon Mr Richmond to repair his horsebox, which had broken down at Drift Bridge. Derek Nimmo accidentally ran his Rolls-Royce into the rear of one of the coaches.

The Company has been featured in several television programmes over the years. In the eighties, Roy Richmond was interviewed live on one of the Company's early morning commuter services. The 'Fergie Tour', a tour of some of the regular places frequented by Sarah Ferguson prior to her marriage to Prince Andrew was also featured on Michael Aspel's, 6 O'clock Show. GMTV also broadcast live from the Epsom Coaches garage one morning regarding the fitment of seat belts on coaches. The Company was used as an example of an operator that had taken the initiative to address the safety belt issue before it became law.

Chapter 8
HORSE TRANSPORT

Although the Company is better known for its coaches, Mr Richmond realised there was a demand for horse transport in the mid 1920's, and he operated a number of horseboxes alongside the charabancs. The local trainers needed to convey their horses from Epsom to the various race meetings.

Richmond's Transport Limited operated in competition with another local family business, Hawkins, for many years. Richmonds had interests in both coaches and horse transport, whilst Hawkins concentrated on horse transport and their Ford commercial dealership. Hawkins now have a Toyota car dealership in Tolworth and Ewell.

Richmond's horseboxes were hired by the local trainers to go to race meetings held at Alexandra Palace, Hurst Park, Kempton Park, Sandown Park, Folkestone, Fontwell, Lingfield, Newbury, Plumpton, Windsor, Wye, as well as many others in the southeast, including Pony Racing at Hawthorn Hill. For longer journeys, horses would be taken to a London terminus and then by rail to the meeting. In those days

Two horseboxes built on the chassis of former Bedford OWB buses – but not those of Epsom Coaches. Some readers may find it interesting to learn that both were built during the Second World War to strictly laid-down government 'austerity' specifications. GZ 2264, on the left, was new to the Northern Ireland Road Transport Board, whilst FRU 152 was new to Pounds of Bournemouth, both in 1943. The latter, at least, was rebuilt as a horsebox in 1949

RICHMONDS TRANSPORT LTD.

(Directors: H. R. Richmond, R. B. Richmond).

Horses carried anywhere in the British Isles.	Horse Transporters 37a SOUTH STREET, EPSOM, SURREY.	Phones: Epsom 555, 3898 (Business Hours). Ewell 4006 (Evenings, etc.)

A letterhead from the late 1940s

it was necessary to load horses at a loading dock as the boxes didn't have the benefit of a ramp. In the early 20's every stable yard and a number of railway stations would have loading docks.

Horseboxes were built on passenger carrying chassis because of their low frame, and a local coachbuilder would build a horsebox to the Richmond's own specification. Horseboxes conveyed three horses, two side-by-side and one between the rear axles, all facing backwards. Roddy Richmond pioneered an articulated unit whereby two horses faced forward and two faced backwards and had the benefit of a very low loading height, ideal for yearlings and two year olds who had not experienced a journey in a horse box before. Roy used to go with his father to the various stables and, on occasions, to meetings.

Between the wars, Roddy Richmond carried horses for Stanley Wootton, Nat Smyth, Harold Wallington, Billy Payne and Tabors at Lower Kingswood. There were two other trainers, Michael Blair at Ewhurst, a director of Stephens Ink, and the actor Tom Walls (who appeared with Ralph Lynn in many comedies at the Aldwych Theatre) at Reigate Road, Ewell. Richmond's conveyed the 1932 Epsom Derby Winner, April the Fifth for Tom Walls.

Whereas Hawkins, the other local horse transporter, had been able to retain most of their horseboxes during the war, Roddy Richmond had all of his requisitioned by the Army. During the latter years of the war, the trainers decided to form a syndicate, and asked Mr Richmond

Bedford horsebox MMO 347, new in May 1956

Two similar Bedfords, that closer to the camera being new in late 1961

to purchase some second-hand horseboxes so that he could recommence business. Following this, his clientele grew considerably to include Ron and Ted Smyth, and their uncle Vic who had well over 100 horses in training between them, Staff Ingham a protégé of Stanley Wootton, Jack Reardon, Johnny Dines, George Duller and Tommy Griffiths accounted for another hundred horses trained locally.

The scene was to change considerably when the rail network was nationalised, as a decision was taken to stop the transport of livestock by rail. Whereas in pre-war days horses were taken to Liverpool Street, Kings Cross, Euston and Esher, Richmond's could now transport horses to all meetings including Aintree, which involved a three-day hire. The going was slow as articulated horseboxes were restricted to 20 mph, and rigid horseboxes to 30 mph.

In addition to race meetings, Richmond's conveyed horses to the bloodstock sales at Newmarket and Ascot. There was also development in the export of thoroughbreds for the bloodstock agencies, and this meant taking horses to the Docks or Airports. Richmond's also conveyed horses from the Royal Stables at Hampton Court and Windsor, mainly for mares in foal.

Drivers were involved with the maintenance of vehicles in those days, especially during the winter months as there was little work. The renewal of matting to the sides of the horse boxes and the replacing of floor boards, together with the painting by hand of the interior and exterior in the familiar red and cream, helped to keep drivers usefully occupied.

Although Richmond's conveyed steeplechasers, most of their business was involved with flat racing, which started in mid-March and finished in early November. There were other journeys to studs, mares in foal, which required the removal of the centre partition, and private sales. Richmond's also transported horses to Bognor Sands, when the frost and snow prevented local training runs.

Trainers, who stabled twenty or more horses, usually employed a Head Lad, and a Travelling Lad. Roy recalls a Travelling Lad who was such a heavy drinker that he was often laid down to recover on a bed of straw for the return journey.

A later Bedford, 1300 KP, new in 1964 posed beside the famous turf
in front of the stands on Epsom Downs.

On Fridays, the Richmond's went to Stebbings, the local paper shop, and bought a copy of the Sporting Handicap. They would go through all the races marking the trainers they did work for. Roy then phoned each one to see whether their entries were taking place, and if they needed transport. Trainers were often out exercising their horses, so they were contacted between their first and second string, usually between 7.30 and 8.30 in the morning when they returned to their Yard. If transport was required, they needed to know whether it was a gelding, colt or filly, so that the box could be loaded accordingly. Orders were never definite until about a day beforehand, and the drivers would have to be visited in the evening to be issued with their instructions, petrol coupons and cash. They would also have to keep the details of the journeys confidential, as tipsters and professional gamblers would make attempts to find out which horses were running.

A typical journey would include one or more of the following - Staff Ingham or Jack Reardon in Ermyn Way, Leatherhead, Johnny Dines at Larchfield on the Headley Road, George Duller in Langley Vale, Harold Wallington, Nat Smyth, Stanley Wootton or Vic Smyths' yards in Treadwell Road and Burgh Heath Road, or Ron Smyth at the top of Andrews Close. A quarter of an hour was allowed between stables, but on occasions it would be extended when a horse was difficult to load, and it then become necessary to phone the next yard to say that they were on their way.

Roy remembers two characters that drove the horseboxes. One driver, Bill Beeching fell over and broke his leg after driving a horsebox to Nottingham, and Roddy, accompanied by Roy, travelled by train to drive the vehicle back home. Bill liked a drink and would normally be found in The Surrey Yeoman, next to his house. Another driver, Mick Dillon, a likeable character, also enjoyed a pint. Mick had a family of four, was always hard up, and before the end of the week would come to Roy for a sub of ten shillings, or a pound. He would say that he needed it to feed the children as the horses had let him down.

The most Richmond's could transport at any one time was 18 horses, so when it came to a local meeting they could cope with as many as 24 horses by operating a

C257 BMG, a 1985 Renault

shuttle service. If there was a duplication of meetings and they had two boxes away, three boxes would be left to shuttle as many as 18 horses to Kempton. Roy tried to increase the number of horses they could carry, by applying to increase the tonnage on their licence, however, Hawkins, their local competitor, managed to successfully block these applications.

Petrol was still rationed in the early post-war years and bunkering fuel was unheard of. Each driver had sufficient Jerricans for the journey. Most drivers would book into digs when away from home, but those who wanted to save on their subsistence, bedded down in the horsebox for the night.

Licensing was the order of the day and Richmond's carried horses under an 'A' licence. Eventually the trainers were bound to obtain their own 'B' licences, so Roddy Richmond decided to sell the horseboxes in 1952, to the same syndicate of trainers that had persuaded him to start up again in 1944.

A contributory factor towards the decision to sell the horse transport business was the constant need to sub-hire, which could mean hiring boxes from as far away as Rottingdean or Datchet. By then, the business had also outgrown its South Street premises and it was decided to concentrate on the coaches.

The horsebox business relocated to The Looe, Reigate Road, Ewell, and then to Betchworth. They are currently trading under the name of Richmond's International Horse Transport, and are based in Cobham. Despite the change of ownership, the family name has been retained, as well as the red and cream colour scheme that the coaches are renowned for. Their business now covers journeys into Europe, mainly working for the Army and the Police, as most trainers have their own transport these days. Modern transporters can now carry an average of nine horses.

Annexe A
COMPANY PERSONNEL – OCTOBER 2002

DIRECTORS
Roy Richmond MBE - Chairman
Doris Richmond
Andrew Richmond - Managing Director / Company Secretary
Rosemary Lever B Sc (Hons)
Steve Whiteway - Commercial Director

MANAGERS
Debbie Bell - Finance
Mike Burnham - Bus Operations
Luis Castanheiro - Bus General
Spencer Green - Epsom Coaches
Alistair Scott - Epsom Holidays
Paul Storey - Service Department

Recognition is also given to the following current full-time members of staff who have completed 10-years or more continuous service as at 1st November 2002

Name	Years service	Name	Years service
Jackie Askins	10	Gary Bishop	14
Justine Sherwood	10	Chris Harding	16
Sarah Agutter	10	Syd Cannon	16
Spencer Green	12	Les Wernham	18
Denis Sainsbury	12	Dave Gettings	20
Steve Harris	13	Tony Hallett	27
Kevin Liquorish	13	Dave Broughton	29
Vivien Elkins	13	John Reeves	29
Trudie Garner	14	Charlie Kingsley	30
Alistair Scott	14	Ivan Stanley	31
Phil Allport	14		

Whilst the above list shows current members of staff with long service, there have been numerous other members of staff that have, in the past, completed ten years or more service. We regret that records are not accurate enough for us to publish a comprehensive list, but we do wish to acknowledge their contribution to the Company.

Annexe B

FLEET LIST – VEHICLES OWNED

The following is a list of buses and coaches owned by the Company since 1920. The list excludes loaned, demonstrated, hired and support vehicles.

Reg'n number	Fleet number	Chassis make	Chassis model	Body make	Body model	Seats	Bought	Notes
?		3 x Thornycroft (purchased, details not known)						
?		A.E.C.						
?		Lancia					1920	
?		Ford	Model T				1921	
PA 9538		Straker Squire		Burtenshaw			1921	
PB 8058		Lancia		Warwick			1921	
PK 1815		Reo					1928	
UU 5955		Albion	PR28				1932	
PK 5568		Lancia					1932	
PK 7883		Albion	PM28	Duple		C31	1932	
PL 503		Gilford	168 OT	Duple		C32	1932	
PJ 4824		Bedford	WLB				1933	
PJ 5953		Bedford	WLB			C20F	1933	
BPG 516		Bedford	WLB	Duple		C20F	1934	
GPC 408		Bedford	WTB	Duple	Hendonian	C25F	1938	
GPE 744		Bedford	WTB	Duple	Hendonian	C25F	1938	
KPA 91		Bedford	OWB	Duple	Utility	UB32F	1944	
KPD 329		Bedford	OB	Duple	Vista	C27F	1946	
LPC 62		Bedford	OB	Duple	Vista	C29F	1947	
LPC 938		Bedford	OB	Duple	Vista	C29F	1947	
FFD 367		Bedford	OWB	Duple	Utility	UB28F	1948	New 1945
MPB 666		Bedford	OB	Duple	Vista	C29F	1948	
MPE 651		Maudslay	Marathon	Whitson		C33F	1948	
MPG 625		Maudslay	Marathon	Whitson		C33F	1948	
MPL 534		Crossley	SD42	Whitson		C33F	1949	
NPA 626		Austin	CXB	Whitson		C29F	1949	
NPB 741		Crossley	SD42	Whitson		C33F	1949	
NPC 416		Bedford	OB	Duple	Vista	C29F	1949	
NPD 239		Bedford	OB	Duple	Vista	C29F	1949	
OPC 286		Bedford	OB	Duple	Vista	C29F	1950	
OPF 331		AEC	Regal 111	Duple		FC35F	1950	
PPF 490		Bedford	SB	Duple	Vega	C33F	1951	
PPF 908		AEC	Regal IV	Whitson		C41C	1951	
PPH 698		Bedford	SBG	Duple	Vega	C33F	1951	
PPJ 333		Maudslay	Marathon	Whitson		C35F	1951	
RPJ 304		AEC	Regal IV	Yeates		C41C	1952	
MXV 73		Bedford	SB	Gurney Nutting		C38F	1952	
RPD 222		Bedford	SB	Gurney Nutting		C33F	1953	New 1951
TPE 550		Bedford	SBG	Yeates	Riviera	C35F	1953	
TPF 332		Bedford	SB	Yeates	Riviera	C35F	1953	
TPL 990		Bedford	SB	Yeates	Riviera	C36F	1954	
VPB 155		AEC	Reliance	Yeates	Riviera	C41C	1954	
VPE 888		Bedford	SBG	Yeates	Riviera 11	C36F	1954	
VPK 500		Bedford	SBG	Yeates	Riviera 11	C36F	1954	
77 EMC		Bedford	SBG	Duple	Super Vega	C38F	1955	
78 EMC		Bedford	SBG	Duple	Super Vega	C38F	1955	

A Thornycroft charabanc belonging to Richmond & Reeves, registration not known

Bedford 29-seater, LPC 62, new in 1947 and seen by the River Thames on Boat Race Day having carried the Cambridge team. Regular drivers on this type of vehicle were Hugh Perry, Ernie Shrubb, Ernie Warwick and Albert Wall

Reg'n. number	Fleet number	Chassis make	Chassis model	Body make	Body model	Seats	Bought	Notes
YPF 70		Bedford	SBG	Yeates	Riviera	C41F	1955	
UPF 668		Bedford	SBG	Duple	Vega	C36F	1956	New 1954
601 BPA		Bedford	SBG	Duple	Super Vega	C41F	1956	
111 CPB		AEC	Reliance	Yeates	Europa	C41F	1957	
590 CPF		Bedford	A4/L7	Plaxton		C29F	1957	
225 DPA		Bedford	SBG	Yeates	Europa	C41F	1957	
715 DPD		Bedford	SB3	Yeates	Europa	C41F	1957	
121 EPL		Bedford	SB8	Duple	Super Vega	C41F	1958	
825 FPJ		Bedford	C4Z2	Duple	Super Vista	C29F	1958	
MUR 204		Maudslay	Marathon	Whitson		C35F	1958	New 1951
80 JPF		Bedford	SB1	Burlingham	Seagull	C41F	1959	
495 KPC		Bedford	SB1	Burlingham	Seagull	C41F	1959	
204 MPG		Bedford	SB8	Duple	Super Vega	C41F	1960	
205 MPG		Bedford	C5Z1	Duple	Super Vista	C29F	1960	
YXH 867		Bedford	SB8	Duple	Super Vega	C41F	1960	
YXH 868		Bedford	C5Z1	Duple	Super Vista	C29F	1960	
261 OPB		Austin	J2VA	Kenex		12	1960	
299 BLB		Bedford	SB1	Duple	Super Vega	C41F	1961	
273 AOU		Bedford	SB8	Duple	Super Vega	C41F	1961	
274 AOU		Bedford	SB8	Duple	Super Vega	C41F	1961	
415 BYR		Karrier	D98A	Plaxton		C14F	1961	
675 CJJ		Bedford	SB1	Duple	Super Vega	C41F	1961	
661 WPE		Bedford	SB5	Duple	Super Vega	C37F	1962	
220 WPL		Bedford	VAS 1	Plaxton	Embassy	C29F	1962	
113 XPA		Bedford	SB5	Duple	Super Vega	C41F	1962	
348 XPJ		AEC	Reliance	Plaxton	Panorama*	C51F	1962	*Continental
469 XPL		AEC	Reliance	Plaxton	Panorama*	C51F	1962	*Continental
LFJ 737		Bedford	SBG	Duple	Vega	C33F	1962	New 1951
4280 PL		Austin	J2BA	B.M.C.		12	1962	
109 LTV		Bedford	SB8	Duple	Super Vega	C41F	1962	New 1961
3242 PJ		Bedford	VAS 1	Plaxton	Embassy	C23F	1963	
4096 PJ		Bedford	VAS 1	Plaxton	Embassy	C23F	1963	
UPL 7		Bedford	SB0	Duple	Vega	C36F	1963	New 1954
TEL 593		Bedford	SBG	Duple	Super Vega	C41F	1963	New 1956
942 AWR		Bedford	SB1	Yeates	Pegasus	DP44F	1963	New 1962
4230 PE		Bedford	VAL 14	Willowbrook		B54F	1964	
100 HOR		Bedford	VAL 14	Duple	Vega Major	C52F	1964	
531 LOR		Bedford	VAL 14	Harrington	Legionnaire	C49F	1964	
532 LOR		Bedford	VAL 14	Harrington	Legionnaire	C49F	1964	
533 LOR		Bedford	VAL 14	Harrington	Legionnaire	C49F	1964	
534 LOR		Bedford	SB5	Plaxton	Embassy IV	C41F	1964	
535 LOR		Bedford	VAL 14	Harrington	Legionnaire	C52F	1964	
536 LOR		Bedford	VAL 14	Harrington	Legionnaire	C52F	1964	
716 CMJ		Bedford	SB1	Duple	Super Vega	C41F	1964	New 1960
826 FMH		Karrier	52A	Reading		C12F	1964	New 1955
537 NHO		Bedford	VAS 1	Plaxton	Embassy	C29F	1964	
538 NHO		Bedford	VAS 1	Plaxton	Embassy	C29F	1964	
AHO 539 C		Bedford	SB5	Plaxton	Embassy IV	C41F	1965	
AHO 540 C		Bedford	SB5	Plaxton	Embassy IV	C41F	1965	
AHO 541 C		Bedford	SB13	Duple	Commander	C37F	1965	
AHO 542 C		Bedford	SB13	Duple	Commander	C37F	1965	
BHO 543 C		Bedford	CALZ30	Martin Walter		11	1965	
BOT 544 C		Bedford	VAL 14	Duple	Vega Major	C52F	1965	
DCG 545 C		Bedford	VAS 1	Plaxton	Embassy IV	C29F	1965	
DHO 546 C		Bedford	VAM 14	Duple	Commander	C41F	1965	
EAA 547 D		Bedford	VAS 1	Plaxton	Embassy IV	C29F	1966	
MPA 550 D		Bedford	VAM 14	Duple	Commander	C41F	1966	

GNM 232N, a 1975 Bristol LHS with 33-seat Plaxton Supreme bodywork

415 BYR was a 1961 Karrier D98A with attractive 14-seat Plaxton coach bodywork

Reg'n. number	Fleet number	Chassis make	Chassis model	Body make	Body model	Seats	Bought	Notes
MPA 551 D		Bedford	VAM 14	Duple	Commander	C41F	1966	
MPA 552 D		Bedford	VAM 14	Duple	Bella Venture	C41F	1966	
FAA 553 D		Bedford	VAM 14	Duple	Commander	C42F	1966	
FAA 554 D		Bedford	VAM 14	Duple	Commander	C42F	1966	
FOU 301 D		Bedford	VAM 14	Duple	Commander	C45F	1966	
HOT 932 E		Ford	Transit	South Hants		12	1967	
JAA 302 E		Bedford	VAM 14	Duple	Commander	C45F	1967	
JAA 303 E		Bedford	VAM 14	Duple	Commander	C45F	1967	
JAA 304 E		Bedford	VAM 14	Duple	Commander	C45F	1967	
JAA 305 E		Bedford	VAM 14	Duple	Commander	C45F	1967	
JAA 548 E		Bedford	VAS 1	Plaxton	Panorama 1	C29F	1967	
JOT 686 E		Ford	Transit	Williams Deansgate		12	1967	
LOR 631 F		Bedford	VAS 5	Plaxton	Panorama 1	C29F	1968	
NOR 632 F		Bedford	VAS 5	Plaxton	Panorama 1	C29F	1968	
NOR 633 F		Bedford	SB5	Plaxton	Panorama 1	C37F	1968	
NOR 634 F		Bedford	SB5	Plaxton	Panorama 1	C37F	1968	
NOR 635 F		Bedford	VAL 70	Plaxton	Panorama 1	C52F	1968	
OJU 636 F		Bedford	VAM 70	Duple	Viceroy	C45F	1968	
LNC 391 G		Ford	Transit	Williams Deansgate		12	1968	
LNE 524 G		Ford	Transit	Williams Deansgate		12	1968	
VYT 491 G		Bedford	VAM 70	Duple	Viceroy	C45F	1969	
VYT 492 G		Bedford	VAM 70	Duple	Viceroy	C45F	1969	
VYT 493 G		Bedford	VAL 70	Duple	Viceroy 37	C53F	1969	
VYT 494 G		Bedford	VAL 70	Duple	Viceroy 37	C53F	1969	
VYT 495 G		Bedford	VAL 70	Duple	Viceroy 37	C53F	1969	
BPJ 555 H		Ford	R192	Plaxton	Elite	C41F	1970	
OTM 526 H		Ford	R226	Plaxton	Elite	C49F	1970	
DPD 556 J		Ford	R192	Plaxton	Elite	C41F	1970	
XOR 470 J		Bedford	YRQ	Plaxton	Elite 2	C41F	1971	
XOT 919 J		Bedford	PJK	Plaxton	Panorama 1	C29F	1971	
XOT 920 J		Bedford	PJK	Plaxton	Panorama 1	C29F	1971	
WUR 859 J		Bedford	PJK	Duple	Vista 25	C29F	1971	
WUR 869 J		Bedford	YRQ	Plaxton	Elite 11	C41F	1971	
WNK 480 J		Ford	R226	Duple	Viceroy	C52F	1971	
SMJ 255 J		Ford	R226	Plaxton	Elite 11	C53F	1971	
XUR 271 J		Seddon	Pennine 4	Plaxton	Elite 11	C53F	1971	
GPG 602 K		Volkswagen		Volkswagen	Microbus	7	1971	
EOR 557 K		Bedford	YRQ	Plaxton	Elite 11	C41F	1972	
EOR 558 K		Bedford	YRQ	Plaxton	Elite 11	C41F	1972	
EOR 559 K		Bedford	YRQ	Plaxton	Elite 11	C41F	1972	
EOR 560 K		Bedford	YRQ	Plaxton	Elite 11	C41F	1972	
FCG 921 K		Bedford	PJK	Plaxton	Panorama	C29F	1972	
FCG 922 K		Bedford	PJK	Plaxton	Panorama	C29F	1972	
FOU 216 K		Ford	Transit	Ford	Transit	12	1972	
JHO 923 L		Bedford	PJK	Duple	Vista 25	C29F	1972	
JHO 924 L		Bedford	PJK	Duple	Vista 25	C29F	1972	
OYL 217 L		Ford	Transit	Ford	Transit	12	1972	
LHO 530 L		Bedford	YRT	Plaxton	Elite 111	C53F	1973	
MCG 531 L		Bedford	YRT	Duple	Dominant	C53F	1973	
MOR 410 L		Bedford	YRQ	Plaxton	Elite 111	C41F	1973	
MOU 532 L		Bedford	YRT	Plaxton	Elite 111	C53F	1973	
MOU 533 L		Bedford	YRT	Plaxton	Elite 111	C53F	1973	
KNR 327 L		Leyland	Leopard PSU5/4R	Plaxton	Elite 111	C53F	1973	
KNR 328 L		Leyland	Leopard PSU5/4R	Plaxton	Elite 111	C53F	1973	
ORO 326 L		Leyland	Leopard PSU5/4R	Plaxton	Elite 111	C57F	1973	
OOU 534 M		Bedford	YRT	Plaxton	Elite 111	C53F	1973	
OOU 535 M		Bedford	YRT	Plaxton	Elite 111	C53F	1973	

Reg'n. number	Fleet number	Chassis make	Chassis model	Body make	Body model	Seats	Bought	Notes
TOT 536 M		Bedford	YRT	Plaxton	Elite 111	C53F	1974	
WJH 322 M		AEC	Reliance	Plaxton	Elite 111	C57F	1974	
WJH 323 M		AEC	Reliance	Plaxton	Elite 111	C57F	1974	
WJH 324 M		AEC	Reliance	Plaxton	Elite 111	C57F	1974	
WJH 325 M		AEC	Reliance	Plaxton	Elite 111	C57F	1974	
HPB 660 N		Bedford	YRQ	Plaxton	Elite 111	C41F	1975	
HPB 661 N		Bedford	YRQ	Plaxton	Elite 111	C41F	1975	
HPB 662 N		Bedford	YRQ	Plaxton	Elite 111	C41F	1975	
HPB 670 N		Bedford	YRT	Plaxton	Elite 111	C53F	1975	
HPB 671 N		Bedford	YRT	Plaxton	Elite 111	C53F	1975	
GNM 232 N		Bristol	LHS6L	Plaxton	Supreme	C33F	1975	
GNM 233 N		Bristol	LHS6L	Plaxton	Supreme	C33F	1975	
GNM 234 N*		Bristol	LHS6L	Plaxton	Supreme	C33F	1975	
KGN 261 N		Bedford	YRT	Plaxton	Elite 111	C53F	1975	
KGT 895 N		Bristol	LHS6L	Plaxton	Supreme	C33F	1975	
NGO 663 P		Bedford	YRQ	Plaxton	Supreme	C41F	1976	
NGP 100 P		Ford	Transit	Williams Deansgate		12	1976	
OGT 329 P		Leyland	Leopard PSU5A/4R	Plaxton	Supreme	C51F	1976	
PGN 320 P		Leyland	Leopard PSU5A/4R	Plaxton	Supreme	C55F	1976	
PGN 321 P		Leyland	Leopard PSU5A/4R	Plaxton	Supreme	C55F	1976	
PGN 330 P		Leyland	Leopard PSU5A/4R	Plaxton	Supreme	C51F	1976	
RGF 230 P		Bristol	LHS6L	Plaxton	Supreme	C33F	1976	
RGF 231 P		Bristol	LHS6L	Plaxton	Supreme	C33F	1976	
SGN 331R		Leyland	Leopard PSU5A/4R	Plaxton	Supreme	C46F	1976	
UGK 228R		Bristol	LHS6L	Plaxton	Supreme	C33F	1977	
UGC 229R*		Bristol	LHS6L	Plaxton	Supreme	C33F	1977	
UGO 318R		Leyland	Leopard PSU5A/4R	Plaxton	Supreme	C55F	1977	
UGO 319R		Leyland	Leopard PSU5A/4R	Plaxton	Supreme	C55F	1977	
VGJ 317R		Leyland	Leopard PSU5A/4R	Plaxton	Supreme	C55F	1977	
VGK 332R		Leyland	Leopard PSU5A/4R	Plaxton	Supreme	C46F	1977	
WGK 316R		Leyland	Leopard PSU5B/4R	Plaxton	Supreme	C55F	1977	
WGK 333R		Leyland	Leopard PSU5B/4R	Plaxton	Supreme	C46F	1977	
BGJ 314S		Leyland	Leopard PSU5C/4R	Plaxton	Supreme	C55F	1978	
BGJ 315S		Leyland	Leopard PSU5C/4R	Plaxton	Supreme	C55F	1978	
CGF 311S		Leyland	Leopard PSU5C/4R	Plaxton	Supreme	C55F	1978	
CGF 312S		Leyland	Leopard PSU5C/4R	Plaxton	Supreme	C55F	1978	
CGF 313S		Leyland	Leopard PSU5C/4R	Plaxton	Supreme	C55F	1978	
EGT 310T		Leyland	Leopard PSU5C/4R	Plaxton	Supreme	C55F	1978	
FGC 309T		Leyland	Leopard PSU5C/4R	Plaxton	Supreme	C55F	1978	
FGJ 308T		Leyland	Leopard PSU5C/4R	Plaxton	Supreme	C55F	1978	
GGF 227T		Bristol	LHS6L	Plaxton	Supreme	C33F	1978	
GGT 334T		Leyland	Leopard PSU5C/4R	Plaxton	Supreme	C50F	1979	
GGT 335T		Leyland	Leopard PSU5C/4R	Plaxton	Supreme	C50F	1979	
HGN 307T		Leyland	Leopard PSU5C/4R	Plaxton	Supreme	C55F	1979	
JGO 336T		Leyland	Leopard PSU5C/4R	Plaxton	Supreme	C50F	1979	
KGF 305T		Leyland	Leopard PSU5C/4R	Plaxton	Supreme	C55F	1979	
KGF 306T		Leyland	Leopard PSU5C/4R	Plaxton	Supreme	C55F	1979	
MGC 337V		Leyland	Leopard PSU5C/4R	Plaxton	Supreme	C50F	1979	
MGC 338V		Leyland	Leopard PSU5C/4R	Plaxton	Supreme	C50F	1979	
OGK 240V		Mercedes	L508D	Reeve Burgess		C18F	1980	
PGC 339V		Leyland	Leopard PSU5C/4R	Plaxton	Supreme	C50F	1980	
PGC 340V		Leyland	Leopard PSU5C/4R	Plaxton	Supreme	C50F	1980	
PGH 341V		Leyland	Leopard PSU5C/4R	Plaxton	Supreme	C50F	1980	
PGO 342V		Leyland	Leopard PSU5C/4R	Plaxton	Supreme	C50F	1980	
SGH 241V		Mercedes	L508D	Reeve Burgess		C18F	1980	
XGO 225W		Bristol	LHS6L	Plaxton	Supreme	C30F	1981	
XGO 226W		Bristol	LHS6L	Plaxton	Supreme	C30F	1981	

Reg'n. number	Fleet number	Chassis make	Chassis model	Body make	Body model	Seats	Bought	Notes
AGJ 343W		Leyland	Tiger TRCTL11/3R	Plaxton	Supreme	C50F	1981	
AGJ 344W		Leyland	Tiger TRCTL11/3R	Plaxton	Supreme	C50F	1981	
BGP 345X		Leyland	Tiger TRCTL11/3R	Plaxton	Supreme	C50F	1981	
GGC 233X		Bristol	LHS6L	Plaxton	Supreme	C30F	1981	
GGC 234X		Bristol	LHS6L	Plaxton	Supreme	C30F	1981	
GGJ 346X		Leyland	Tiger TRCTL11/3R	Plaxton	Supreme	C50F	1982	
GGJ 347X		Leyland	Tiger TRCTL11/3R	Plaxton	Supreme	C50F	1982	
NGT 1Y		Volvo	B10M GT	Plaxton	Paramount 3500	C44FT	1983	
NGT 2Y		Volvo	B10M GT	Plaxton	Paramount 3500	C44FT	1983	
NGT 303Y		Volvo	B10M GT	Plaxton	Paramount 3500	C50F	1983	
NGT 304Y		Volvo	B10M GT	Plaxton	Paramount 3500	C50F	1983	
A400 WGH		Volvo	B10M GLT	Plaxton	Paramount 3500	C40FT	1984	
A401 WGH		Volvo	B10M GLT	Plaxton	Paramount 3500	C40FT	1984	
A500 WGH		Volvo	B10M GLT	Plaxton	Paramount 3500	C50F	1984	
A501 WGH		Volvo	B10M GLT	Plaxton	Paramount 3500	C50F	1984	
A502 WGH		Volvo	B10M GLT	Plaxton	Paramount 3500	C50F	1984	
A503 WGH		Volvo	B10M GLT	Plaxton	Paramount 3500	C50F	1984	
A236 EPA		Volkswagen		Volkswagen	Microbus	7	1984	
B504 CGP		Volvo	B10M GT	Plaxton	Paramount 3200	C50F	1985	
B505 CGP		Volvo	B10M GT	Plaxton	Paramount 3200	C50F	1985	
B506 CGP		Volvo	B10M GT	Plaxton	Paramount 3200	C50F	1985	
B507 CGP		Volvo	B10M GT	Plaxton	Paramount 3200	C50F	1985	
B508 CGP		Volvo	B10M GT	Plaxton	Paramount 3200	C50F	1985	
C200 HGF		Mercedes	L608D	Plaxton	Mini Supreme	C20F	1985	
C360 HGF		Volvo	B9M-46	Plaxton	Paramount 3200	C36F	1985	
C361 HGF		Volvo	B9M-46	Plaxton	Paramount 3200	C36F	1985	
C509 HGF		Volvo	B10M-61	Plaxton	Paramount 3200	C50F	1985	
C201 KGJ		Mercedes	L608D	Plaxton	Mini Supreme	C20F	1986	
C510 LGH		Volvo	B10M-61	Plaxton	Paramount 3200	C50F	1986	
C511 LGH		Volvo	B10M-61	Plaxton	Paramount 3200	C50F	1986	
D202 PGJ		Mercedes	L608D	Plaxton	Mini Supreme	C20F	1986	
D203 RGH		Volkswagen	LT55	Optare	City Pacer	B25F	1987	
D600 RGJ		Bedford	YMT	Plaxton	Derwent	B53F	1987	
D601 RGJ		Bedford	YMT	Plaxton	Derwent	B53F	1987	
D602 RGJ		Bedford	YMT	Plaxton	Derwent	B53F	1987	
D603 RGJ		Bedford	YMT	Plaxton	Derwent	B53F	1987	
D604 RGJ		Bedford	YMT	Plaxton	Derwent	B53F	1987	
E204 YGC		Mercedes	709D	Plaxton	Beaver	C25F	1988	
E205 YGC		Mercedes	709D	Plaxton	Beaver	C25F	1988	
E512 YGC		Volvo	B10M-61	Van Hool	Alizee H	C49FT	1988	
E513 YGC		Volvo	B10M-61	Van Hool	Alizee H	C49FT	1988	
E514 YGC		Volvo	B10M-61	Van Hool	Alizee H	C49FT	1988	
E515 YGC		Volvo	B10M-61	Van Hool	Alizee H	C49FT	1988	
E206 BGN		Mercedes	709D	Plaxton	Beaver	DP25F	1988	
F207 DGT		Mercedes	709D	Plaxton	Beaver	DP25F	1988	
F208 GGH		Mercedes	709D	Robin Hood		B26F	1988	
F209 GGH		Mercedes	709D	Robin Hood		B26F	1988	
F691 MPF		Volkswagen	Devon	Microbus		11	1988	
F864 SPC		Volkswagen	Devon	Microbus		11	1989	
F516 GGJ		Volvo	B10M-60	Van Hool	Alizee H	C53F	1989	
F517 GGJ		Volvo	B10M-60	Van Hool	Alizee H	C53F	1989	
G518 OGP		Volvo	B10M-60	Van Hool	Alizee H	C53F	1990	
G519 OGP		Volvo	B10M-60	Van Hool	Alizee H	C53F	1990	
H210 UGO		Mercedes	709D	Phoenix		B26F	1990	
H531 WGH		Volvo	B10M-60	Van Hool	Alizee H	C53F	1991	
H532 WGH		Volvo	B10M-60	Van Hool	Alizee H	C53F	1991	
H533 WGH		Volvo	B10M-60	Van Hool	Alizee H	C53F	1991	
F670 NPG		Mercedes	811D	Optare	Star Rider	B33F	1991	New 1988

Reg'n. number	Fleet number	Chassis make	Chassis model	Body make	Body model	Seats	Bought	Notes
C331 DND		Volvo	B10M-61	Van Hool	Alizee H	C53F	1992	New 1986
C529 DND		Volvo	B10M-61	Van Hool	Alizee H	C53F	1992	New 1986
J721 FGP		Toyota	HDB30R	Caetano	Optimo 11	C18F	1992	
K460 PNR		Toyota	HDB30R	Caetano	Optimo 11	C18F	1992	
K892 CSX		Dennis	Dart	Alexander	Dash	B40F	1988	
K593 BEG		Mercedes	709D	Marshall		B27F	1992	
K288 GDT		Volvo	B10M-60	Van Hool	Alizee H	C49FT	1993	Also reg A8 HRR
K289 GDT		Volvo	B10M-60	Van Hool	Alizee H	C49FT	1993	Also reg A9 HRR
K112 NGK		Dennis	Dart	Plaxton	Pointer	B40F	1993	
K113 NGK	LD13	Dennis	Dart	Plaxton	Pointer	B40F	1993	
K465 PNR		Toyota	HDB30R	Caetano	Optimo 11	C18F	1993	Also reg A8 HRR
K321 GEW		Dennis	Dart	Marshall		B40F	1993	
L894 NAV		Mercedes	709D	Marshall		B27F	1993	
L231 BUT		Dennis	Javelin 240	Plaxton	Premiere 320	C53F	1994	
L232 BUT		Dennis	Javelin 240	Plaxton	Premiere 320	C53F	1994	
L233 BUT		Dennis	Javelin 240	Plaxton	Premiere 320	C53F	1994	
L234 BUT		Dennis	Javelin 240	Plaxton	Premiere 320	C53F	1994	
M960 CGF	LD14	Dennis	Dart	Plaxton	Pointer	B40F	1994	
M790 LPH		Dennis	Javelin 240	Plaxton	Premiere 320	C53F	1995	
M791 LPH		Dennis	Javelin 240	Plaxton	Premiere 320	C48FT	1995	
M792 LPH		Dennis	Javelin 240	Plaxton	Premiere 320	C48FT	1995	Also reg A9 HRR
M793 LPH		Dennis	Javelin 240	Plaxton	Premiere 320	C53F	1995	
M332 MPG		Dennis	Javelin 240	Plaxton	Premiere 320	C53F	1995	
N401 SPA	LD16	Dennis	Dart	Plaxton	Pointer	B40F	1995	
N402 SPA	LD17	Dennis	Dart	Plaxton	Pointer	B40F	1995	
N405 SPC		Dennis	Javelin 240	Plaxton	Premiere 320	C48FT	1996	Also reg A6 HRR and N678 JGP
N406 SPC	702	Dennis	Javelin GX	Plaxton	Premiere 320	C48FT	1996	
N407 SPC	703	Dennis	Javelin GX	Plaxton	Premiere 320	C53F	1996	
N408 SPC	704	Dennis	Javelin GX	Plaxton	Premiere 320	C53F	1996	
N409 SPC	705	Dennis	Javelin GX	Plaxton	Premiere 320	C53F	1996	
N479 VPA	706	Dennis	Javelin GX	Plaxton	Premiere 320	C53F	1996	
P570 APJ		Mercedes	709D	Plaxton	Beaver	B27F	1996	
H947 JPA		Mercedes	709D	Plaxton	Beaver	B25F	1997	New 1991
P707 DPA	707	Dennis	Javelin GX	Plaxton	Premiere 320	C53F	1997	
P708 DPA	708	Volvo	B10M-62	Jonckheere	Mistral 50	C53F	1997	
P709 DPA	709	Volvo	B10M-62	Jonckheere	Mistral 50	C53F	1997	
P710 DPA	710	Volvo	B10M-62	Jonckheere	Mistrla 50	C53F	1997	
P806 DPA	806	Volvo	B10M-62	Jonckheere	Mistral 50	C49F	1997	
P807 DPA	807	Volvo	B10M-62	Jonckheere	Mistral 50	C49F	1997	
H679 YGO		Optare	MR03	Optare	Metrorider	B26F	1997	New 1991
H680 YGO		Optare	MR03	Optare	Metrorider	B26F	1997	New 1991
H681 YGO		Optare	MR03	Optare	Metrorider	B26F	1997	New 1991
H682 YGO		Optare	MR03	Optare	Metrorider	B26F	1997	New 1991
H683 YGO		Optare	MR03	Optare	Metrorider	B26F	1997	New 1991
H684 YGO		Optare	MR03	Optare	Metrorider	B26F	1997	New 1991
H685 YGO		Optare	MR03	Optare	Metrorider	B26F	1997	New 1991
H686 YGO		Optare	MR03	Optare	Metrorider	B26F	1997	New 1991
H687 YGO		Optare	MR03	Optare	Metrorider	B26F	1997	New 1991
H688 YGO		Optare	MR03	Optare	Metrorider	B26F	1997	New 1991
H689 YGO		Optare	MR03	Optare	Metrorider	B26F	1997	New 1991
R711 KGK	711	Dennis	Javelin GX	Berkhof	Radial	C53F	1998	
R712 KGK	712	Dennis	Javelin GX	Berkhof	Radial	C53F	1998	
R713 KGK	713	Dennis	Javelin GX	Berkhof	Radial	C53F	1998	
R714 KGK	714	Dennis	Javelin GX	Berkhof	Radial	C53F	1998	
R211 MGT		Mercedes	O810D	UVG	Citistar	B27F	1997	
R212 MGT		Mercedes	O810D	UVG	Citistar	B27F	1997	
R213 MGT		Mercedes	O810D	UVG	Citistar	B27F	1997	

Reg'n. number	Fleet number	Chassis make	Chassis model	Body make	Body model	Seats	Bought	Notes
A301XWF		Bedford	YMP	Plaxton	Supreme	C35F	1998	New 1983
S451 LGN	MB15	Mercedes	O814D	Plaxton	Beaver 2	B27F	1998	
S452 LGN	MB16	Mercedes	O814D	Plaxton	Beaver 2	B27F	1998	
S453 LGN	MB17	Mercedes	O814D	Plaxton	Beaver 2	B27F	1998	
S454 LGN	MB18	Mercedes	O814D	Plaxton	Beaver 2	B27F	1998	
S455 LGN	MB19	Mercedes	O814D	Plaxton	Beaver 2	B27F	1998	
S456 LGN	SD10	Dennis	Dart SLF	Plaxton	Mini Pointer	B29F	1999	
S457 LGN	SD11	Dennis	Dart SLF	Plaxton	Mini Pointer	B29F	1999	
S458 LGN	SD12	Dennis	Dart SLF	Plaxton	Mini Pointer	B29F	1999	
S459 LGN	SD13	Dennis	Dart SLF	Plaxton	Mini Pointer	B29F	1999	
S460 LGN	SD14	Dennis	Dart SLF	Plaxton	Mini Pointer	B29F	1999	
S461 LGN	SD15	Dennis	Dart SLF	Plaxton	Mini Pointer	B29F	1999	
S462 LGN	SD16	Dennis	Dart SLF	Plaxton	Mini Pointer	B29F	1999	
S463 LGN	SD17	Dennis	Dart SLF	Plaxton	Mini Pointer	B29F	1999	
S464 LGN	SD18	Dennis	Dart SLF	Plaxton	Mini Pointer	B29F	1999	
S465 LGN	SD19	Dennis	Dart SLF	Plaxton	Mini Pointer	B29F	1999	
S466 LGN	SD20	Dennis	Dart SLF	Plaxton	Mini Pointer	B29F	1999	
T808 TGP	808	Dennis	Javelin GX	Berkhof	Axial	C49FT	1999	
T467 EGT		Dennis	Dart SLF	Plaxton	Pointer 10.1 mtr	B33F	1999	
T468 EGT		Dennis	Dart SLF	Plaxton	Pointer 10.1 mtr	B33F	1999	
T715 GGT	715	Dennis	Javelin GX	Berkhof	Radial	C53F	1999	
V511MGO	501	Iveco	CC80E18M/P	Indcar	Maxim	C27F	2000	
V943 DNB	SD22	Dennis	Dart SLF	Plaxton	Mini Pointer	B29F	2000	
W813 AAY	502	Iveco	CC80E18M/P	Indcar	Maxim	C27F	2000	
G47 TGW		Dennis	Dart	Carlyle		DP28F	2000	New 1990
W871 VGT	SD23	Dennis	Dart SLF	Alexander	8.9 mtr	B29F	2000	
W872 VGT	SD24	Dennis	Dart SLF	Alexander	8.9 mtr	B28F	2000	
W873 VGT	SD25	Dennis	Dart SLF	Alexander	8.9 mtr	B28F	2000	
W874 VGT	SD26	Dennis	Dart SLF	Alexander	8.9 mtr	B28F	2000	
W875 VGT	SD27	Dennis	Dart SLF	Alexander	8.9 mtr	B28F	2000	
W876 VGT	SD28	Dennis	Dart SLF	Alexander	8.9 mtr	B28F	2000	
W877 VGT	809	Volvo	B10M-62	Plaxton	Panther	C49FT	2000	
W878 VGT	810	Volvo	B10M-62	Plaxton	Panther	C49FT	2000	
SN51 UCH	SD31	Dennis	Dart	Plaxton	Pointer	B29F	2001	
SN51 UCJ	SD32	Dennis	Dart	Plaxton	Pointer	B29F	2001	
SN51 UCL	SD30	Dennis	Dart	Plaxton	Pointer	B29F	2001	
SN51 UCM	SD29	Dennis	Dart	Plaxton	Pointer	B29F	2001	
SN51 UCO	SD33	Dennis	Dart	Plaxton	Pointer	B29F	2001	
SN51 UCP	SD34	Dennis	Dart	Plaxton	Pointer	B29F	2001	
SN51 UCR	SD35	Dennis	Dart	Plaxton	Pointer	B29F	2001	
SN51 UCS	SD36	Dennis	Dart	Plaxton	Pointer	B29F	2001	
T75 JBA	SD21	Dennis	Dart SLF	Plaxton	Pointer	B29F	2001	New 1999
LB51 LWN	407	VW	Caravelle	VW	Caravelle	7	2001	
LB51 OCF	401	VW	Caravelle	VW	Caravelle	7	2001	
LB51 OCG	403	VW	Caravelle	VW	Caravelle	7	2001	
LB51 OCH	402	VW	Caravelle	VW	Caravelle	7	2001	
LB51 OCK	405	VW	Caravelle	VW	Caravelle	7	2001	
LB51 OCL	406	VW	Caravelle	VW	Caravelle	7	2001	
LB51 OCR	404	VW	Caravelle	VW	Caravelle	7	2001	
LB51 UFS	408	VW	Caravelle	VW	Caravelle	7	2001	
LB51 UFU	409	VW	Caravelle	VW	Caravelle	7	2001	
T76 JBA	SD37	Dennis	Dart SLF	Plaxton	Pointer	B29FT	2002	New 1999
BX02 CMO		Setra	S315GTHD			C48FT	2002	
BX02 CMU		Setra	S315GTHD			C48FT	2002	

* The chassis from GNM 232N was re-bodied following an accident, and re-registered UGC 229R.

The fleet numbers shown against coaches and buses were first applied in December 1996 and January 2002 respectively.

This fleet list has been compiled from the Company's own records and checked by Maurice Doggett against the records of the PSV Circle to whom due acknowledgement is given.